T0296013

A Study of Risky Business Outcomes

EMERALD STUDIES IN GLOBAL STRATEGIC RESPONSIVENESS

Series Editor: Torben Juul Andersen

Recent Books in Series:

The Responsive Global Organization: New Insights From Global Strategy and International Business
Edited by Torben Juul Andersen

Strategic Responsiveness and Adaptive Organizations: New Research Frontiers in International Strategic Management
Edited by Torben Juul Andersen, Simon Torp, and Stefan Linder

Adapting to Environmental Challenges: New Research in Strategy and International Business
Edited by Torben Juul Andersen and Simon Sunn Torp

Strategic Responses for a Sustainable Future: New Research in International Management
Edited by Torben Juul Andersen

Navigating Corporate Cultures From Within: Making Sense of Corporate Values Seen From an Employee Perspective
By Michael Jakobsen and Verner D. Worm

Responding to Uncertain Conditions: New Research on Strategic Adaptation
By Torben Juul Anderson

A Study of Risky Business Outcomes: Adapting to Strategic Disruption

BY

TORBEN JUUL ANDERSEN

Copenhagen Business School, Denmark

United Kingdom – North America – Japan – India – Malaysia – China

Emerald Publishing Limited
Emerald Publishing, Floor 5, Northspring, 21-23 Wellington Street, Leeds LS1 4DL.

First edition 2023

Reprints and permissions service
Contact: www.copyright.com

British Library Cataloguing in Publication Data
A catalogue record for this book is available from the British Library

ISBN: 978-1-83797-075-9 (Print)
ISBN: 978-1-83797-074-2 (Online)
ISBN: 978-1-83797-076-6 (Epub)

INVESTOR IN PEOPLE

Table of Contents

List of Figures and Tables

Figures

Tables

About the Author

Torben Juul Andersen is Professor of Strategy and International Management and Director of the Global Strategic Responsiveness Initiative, Department of International Economics, Government and Business at the Copenhagen Business School, Denmark.

Preface

More than five years ago, we were contemplating the need for further studies to help us better understand how organizations, or firms, respond to rapidly changing environmental conditions often interrupted by extreme unexpected events. Indeed, the beginnings of the *Emerald Studies in Global Strategic Responsiveness* book series emerged from a similar urge to uncover how responsive global organizations could adjust and adapt their business operations across multiple overseas markets as they deal with unpredictable changes in the turbulent reality that describes the global marketplace.

In recent years, we have seen these turbulent conditions excel as international business activities have been affected by several abrupt and largely unexpected disruptive incidents including a pandemic, a major military conflict, and mounting geopolitical tensions. Hence, we have observed a general development toward global business contexts characterized by radical uncertainty with many unknown factors in play that call for new and more effective ways to deal with the changing risk landscape. As the recent incidents of pandemic and war have demonstrated, most institutions were not prepared for the ensuing chaotic, uncoordinated, and somewhat divergent approaches adopted typically influenced by national political interests. Hence, we continue as societies to struggle with ways to deal with the severe economic ramifications imposed by these events including the formation of resilient global supply-chains in a world of increasing regional tensions while dampening the intermediate effects of inflationary pressures not seen for decades. In short, the challenges foreseen a few years back have not diminished but have rather exacerbated.

Back then, we noted how organizations operating in the global economy were exposed to a daunting array of possible risk events including fiscal crisis, cyberattack, social instability, governance failure, and an increasing frequency of extreme weather incidents. In view of these challenges, some organizations were noted as adjusting better to the changing conditions and thriving under adverse odds whereas many others, maybe most, had a hard time adjusting. This fundamental issue inspired the formulation of a research project attempting to better understand how the observed performance differences were related to strategic response capabilities and expected adaptive outcomes. It was observed as a regular empirical artifact that over given time periods several firms would outperform their peers competing under comparable business conditions and generate favorable performance outcomes whereas a vast number of the firms seemed to produce often extremely poor financial returns. While these extreme occurrences often are overlooked in mainstream management studies, we thought they might provide some interesting insights. Hence, we attempted to study this phenomenon closer to gain more insights about how competing firms and organizations respond and adapt when they are exposed to adverse conditions that at times are inflicted in the form of sudden unexpected events. So, the project attempted to fill an apparent gap in our understanding of how the common contours of realized economic performance come about.

Other motivations include the seeming increase in extreme environmental events of various kinds that generate many surprising disruptions and strategic discontinuities that largely went unnoticed before. This means that contemporary business environments present complex and dynamic contexts where many extreme events may arise that are difficult to predict and therefore notoriously hard to respond to. Hence, it may be difficult for otherwise successful firms to observe ongoing changes and orchestrate effective responses to major shifts in the competitive environment, which in turn may have an adverse effect on their economic fortunes. These characteristics could explain the observed performance data of few over-performers and many underperformers. They also accentuate concerns for strategic adaptation whereby organizations can adjust to gain a better fit with the changing business environment over time where we need a better understanding of the adaptive processes that may lead to the extreme observed outcomes. Hence, the study aimed to develop a deeper understanding of the phenomenon with few high-performers and many extreme negative outcomes typically observed in the empirical data. The insights derived from the study should ideally help organizations increase their awareness of strategic adaptation and improve their response capabilities to gain better adaptive outcomes with stronger performance avoiding downside losses while thriving from an ability to exploit emerging opportunities.

This four-year research effort eventually received financial support from the Independent Research Fund Denmark (Danmarks Frie Forskningsråd Grant #8019-00046B) with the formal title: Risky Business – Managing in a world with extreme exposures (2019–2022). We acknowledge and appreciate this support that made the ensuing reporting of findings possible.

The project name, Risky Business, also the title of a (famed) Tom Cruise movie (1983), and as the movie hints, risky events and circumstances also present opportunities, even if partially self-inflicted, but we know too little about how firms can take on risky initiatives and exploit them to their advantage as the external circumstances change. So, the research project was inspired by an urge to better understand the regularly observed fat-tailed distributions of financial returns across firms, where many of them underperform but a few excel displaying higher performance with lower performance risk. Hence, implicit in this effort was an aim to better understand why some firms appear to adapt rather well to extreme exposures consistently outperforming their peers in the industry when many more of the firms underperform with a substantial number of them posting extreme negative returns.

The project collected extensive datasets for all registered European and North American firms over the 25-year period 1995–2019 which spans diverse economic scenarios of global expansion, recession, and recovery up until the COVID-19 pandemic in 2020. The analyses of both datasets reproduce the extreme left-skewed performance distributions with small positive tails of high-performers across different geographies, industrial sectors, and time intervals. More refined analyses of complete datasets show how the left-skewed returns are associated with negative risk-return relations as high-performers generate superior average returns at lower variation in returns. It is further shown that unfavorable risk-return outcomes are related to overconfident executives whereas high-performers retain a high degree of investment flexibility.

These results resonate with propositions arguing for the advantages of interactive decision-making processes where executives use frequent dispersed insights to update ongoing strategy deliberations expressed in a quantitative model. This strategic responsiveness model is used as a basis to perform computational simulations that show how it can produce empirically observed negatively skewed performance distributions and inverse risk-return relationships. Hence, the studies altogether indicate that interactive collaborative decision-making processes can drive effective strategic adaptation to extreme exposures.

The book presents some of the key findings from this four-year research program conducted between 2019 and 2022 investigating the commonly observed left-skewed distributions of financial returns based on reported accounting performance.

As international economic actors struggle to make necessary adjustments that align their transnational production structures and global value-chains with the evolving political reality, it is clear that multinational organizations must improve their ability to deal with uncertainty and abrupt events. This also includes concerns about increasing demands to deal with potentially extreme weather effects from climate change influenced by ongoing degradation of the natural environment, for example, CO_2 emissions, waste, and pollution. Hence, it is becoming apparent that organizations are incapable of resolving these challenges on their own but require collaborative solutions for sustainable long-term outcomes. We hope that this monograph of sequentially ordered book chapters provides relevant insights to current thinking about strategic adaptation, needed response capabilities, and the formation of resilient organizations within the global economic systems.

The nine chapters that constitute this monograph are included as standalone contributions although they emerge as sequential presentations much in line with the planned progression of the research project. This should provide for flexible use of individual chapters while presenting progressing insights that lead to a conclusion to the extent such is possible. Nonetheless, we hope this can contribute with some interesting and insightful reading.

Torben Juul Andersen
Frederiksberg, March 18, 2023

Chapter 1

Managing (in) a Disruptive World

Abstract

The global environments that surround contemporary business activities are uncertain, fast-changing, and frequently exposed to abrupt unexpected events with the potential to inflict extreme impacts where the ability to respond and adapt the organization effectively becomes a primary strategic concern. However, various firms that operate across diverse industry contexts approach this adaptive challenge in distinct ways that lead to quite diverse outcomes with many negative performers and some high performers with positive risk features. The heterogeneous approaches appear to consistently form extreme left-tailed performance distributions with inverse risk-return features but we are not really able to explain why and how these regularly observed phenomena come about. Hence, we want to study these organizational artifacts by collecting an extensive updated dataset to test the proposed relationships, explore alternative explanations, and learn from the extreme exemplars often referred to as outliers. There are extensive literatures in (strategic) management and finance that have dealt with the distribution of firm returns from slightly different angles but with some emerging commonalities that can inspire further analyses of the performance data. As a precursor for this, we discuss the odds of effective strategic adaptation in complex dynamic environments and introduce resilience as a proper outcome when simple solutions are scarce, and consider conditions that may facilitate these aims. The premises for the ensuing analyses are laid out and the main contents of the following chapters are presented.

Keywords: Extreme events; flexibility; performance outcomes; randomness; response capabilities; strategic adaptation

A Study of Risky Business Outcomes: Adapting to Strategic Disruption, 1–13
Copyright © 2023 by Torben Juul Andersen
Published under exclusive licence by Emerald Publishing Limited
doi:10.1108/978-1-83797-074-220231001

Introduction

Contemporary firms are exposed to a variety of developments and events some of which are hard to predict and may significantly affect performance outcomes. To the extent organizations engage in, or depend on international business activities, the portfolio of potential risk events is even increased exponentially. Companies that maintain operations in different multinational locations engage in various cross-border transactions and confront a complex set of economic, political, and social risk factors that permeate the global economy. This complex dynamic setting gives rise to a multitude of incidents that (often) arise with abrupt unexpected intensity, as noted over recent decades, to inflict (potentially) extreme adverse economic effects. The most impactful of these events constitute non-insurable incidents that are hard to quantify and assign meaningful probabilities to. This includes some of the recently experienced phenomena, such as, global financial crisis, pandemic, military conflict, geopolitical tensions, climate change, and extreme weather events (World Economic Forum, 2022). As a common denominator for these occurrences, they all have general socioeconomic impacts that affect all types of organizational activities both public and private at the same time and thereby have the potential to assume catastrophic dimensions where outcomes are hard to predict as they are influenced by many complex interrelated factors.

Organizations pursue their own individual strategic objectives and adopt different leadership approaches and structural features to accomplish their aims. It should not really surprise us, therefore, that organizations deal with abrupt environmental changes in quite distinct ways and respond to them differently and with highly diverse outcomes. That is, some (maybe few) organizations show an ability to adapt activities and thrive their business against adversities whereas many (possibly most) are less favorable and eventually fail (e.g., Van der Vegt, Essens, Wahlström, & George, 2015). In other words, the effects of heterogeneous abilities of firms to deal with rapid changes have diverse outcomes commensurate with a left-skewed distribution where many firms record mediocre, or negative returns with some high performers. Hence, a fraction of firms seem able to adapt to the changing circumstances and generate superior results.

An organizational ability to consistently outperform over longer periods of time is often referred to as sustainable competitive advantage and is frequently applied to characterize performance by firms that pursue effective adaptive strategies. Nonetheless, the observed results of the concept appear to represent a relatively rare and fleeting phenomenon that only prevails over shorter periods of time. Hence, a typical observation from realized performance data is that a vast number of firms perform relatively poorly expressed in a left-skewed tail of underperformers with some outliers that show extreme negative returns (e.g., Bloom & Reenen, 2007). Empirical examinations of realized economic returns quite consistently show that many firms underperform while some outperform their industry peers and display favorable risk-return outcomes in given time intervals (e.g., Andersen, Denrell, & Bettis, 2007).

These negatively skewed performance distributions typically violate the Gaussian normality features assumed in conventional statistical methods including commonly adopted linear regression analysis (e.g., Baum & McKelvey, 2006). It is also a challenge to statistical analyses applied in dynamic factor and vector-autoregressive models used to analyze longitudinal relationships. The left-skewed tails of underperformers attest to the difficulty otherwise successful firms may have in orchestrating effective responses to ongoing changes and major shifts in the competitive environment where some may end up in the negative performance tail (Fig. 1.1). Empirical data studies typically manage these outliers by applying automated screening techniques that cut-off the extreme observations in a sample that violate the nice features of a normal distribution. However, this may overlook important aspects of firm performance where outliers both in the negative and positive tails of the distribution could help uncover (new) and relevant insights (e.g., Boisot & McKelvey, 2011; Taleb, 2007).

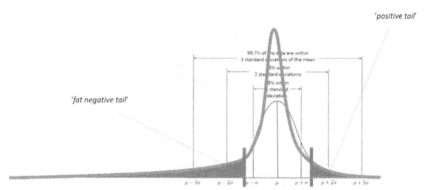

Fig. 1.1.   A Display of (Extreme) Negative Outliers and Some Positive Outliers.

Given the frequent use of semiautomated approaches to eliminate the outlier phenomenon,[1] we tend to ignore (potentially) important aspects of the empirical evidence and as a consequence, we are (really) unable to explain how, and why, the often-observed negatively skewed performance distributions arise. We are also short of plausible explanations for the (related) inverse risk-return characteristics observed in the standard accounting-based financial return measures. That is, we cannot really explain seemingly essential "empirical regularities" observed in the real-world performance data (Helfat, 2007). This identifies a need to (better)

---

[1]A common approach is to eliminate all observations that fall below the mean value (μ) minus three times the standard deviation (3σ) and above the mean value plus three standard deviations (see Fig. 1.1). Provided the data follow a normal distribution, it means that "extreme" values falling beyond the lower and upper limits cut off 1.5 per-mille of the observations on either side of the distribution. However, if the distribution is leptokurtic and very left-skewed there can be a substantially higher share of outliers particularly in the left tail.

understand how these regularly observed empirical phenomena arise while investigating central factors that influence performance outcomes and their relative position in the performance distribution.

Further exploratory studies of response models and behavioral traits as well as actions pursued by negative and positive outliers may generate interesting insights that can help us (better) understand why some organizations show more or less effective adaptive outcomes. The real data seem to indicate that only some organizations are able to thrive against adversity whereas a majority of firms are challenged by emergent environmental events and underperform. We would like to better comprehend what may cause these differences in outcomes, so the ensuing chapters present different exploratory analyses pursued to fill this apparent knowledge gap.

General Background

One view on the left-skewed performance outcomes is that it might reflect poor adaptation to changing competitive conditions that leave some firms in an outdated position in terms of living up to the current demands in the market. Adapting the strategic position of the firm to provide a better fit with prevailing conditions in the business environment is a rather old perspective that can be traced in the management field for more than 30 years (Andersen, 2015a). Yet, we still know little to explain how organizational adaptation processes among firms lead to the extreme left-skewed outcomes observed in the performance distributions. The ensuing chapters will attempt to gain more detailed insights about this phenomenon and create a better understanding of the dynamic processes that lead to few high performers and many negative performers as observed empirically. The acquired insights might help organizations refine their adaptive processes and improve performance outcomes by avoiding downside losses, reducing excessive adjustment costs, while thriving on opportunities that can redesign the business and enhance its value-creating potential.

The observation that some firms outperform within given time-periods and display favorable risk-return outcomes in the context of an erratic environment with large exposures is a real empirical artifact (e.g., Andersen et al., 2007; Bromiley, 1991a, 1991b). The ability to increase performance and reduce risk at the same time as expressed in negative risk-return correlations reflects the so-called "Bowman paradox" where high average returns was found associated with low variance in returns (Bowman, 1980). It is referred to as a "paradox" because it was a controversial finding at odds with conventional assumptions in the finance field (Fig. 1.2).

There was a general belief that financial assets priced on liquid exchanges would fall along a capital market line showing a positive relationship between the perceived risk and the required rate of return expressed as a premium above the risk-free rate (Sharpe, 1964). This is the basis for the so-called capital asset pricing model (CAPM) that continues to prevail in present-day corporate finance applications. Part of the explanation for the noted difference relates to the fact that the management studies adopt an *ex post* return construct that reflects realized

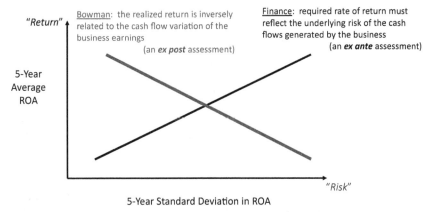

Fig. 1.2.   Two Views of the Relationship Between Performance (Return) and Risk.

accounting performance whereas finance adopts an ex ante return construct that reflects the return required by investors to accept the perceived risk of the traded asset. We discuss these conceptual differences further in Chapter 5. The phenomenon observed by Bowman (1980) over given time-periods can be explained by the effects of organizational adaptation processes where the competing firms display differences in their ability to respond to major environmental changes. How this may come about through different longitudinal relationships between firm performance and risk propensity is the topic of a rather diverse range of research streams that will be discussed in more detail in later chapters.

Andersen et al. (2007) used empirical analyses, computational simulations, and mathematical derivations to show that heterogeneous abilities of firms to respond to frequent environmental changes can lead to negatively skewed *ex post* performance outcomes with inverse risk-return conditions. That is, for a given state of the economy, firms with superior adaptive capabilities will lead to favorable risk-return outcomes with many firms showing adverse results. Hence, those performance distributions that display negatively skewed outcomes are closely associated with the inverse risk-return characteristics (e.g., Andersen & Bettis, 2014; Henkel, 2009). However, there is little evidence that firms with effective strategic adaptation and superior performance prevail for extended periods as the favorable risk-return outcomes show diminishing effects as time-lags are increased (Andersen & Bettis, 2015). This may support the claims that the ability to conduct effective adaptive responses as the means to gain sustainable advantage is a rather fleeting phenomenon where organizations, leaders, and governance systems may face (at times) quite dramatic reshufflings as time goes by.

Resilient recovery from sudden incidents and environmental changes appears associated with decentralized engagement where dispersed entities and managers respond to emerging events (Van der Vegt, Essens, Wahlström, & George, 2015). This may combine central reasoning with delegation of decision power corresponding to an interactive strategy-making approach (e.g., Andersen, 2015b) where adaptive capabilities seem to thrive on entrepreneurial initiatives that may contravene the official strategy (e.g., Bower & Gilbert, 2005; Burgelman, 1983, 1996). Hence, interacting information processing between slow-structured analyses at the center and fast-dispersed initiatives around the periphery may form an effective organizational response dynamic (e.g., Andersen & Fredens, 2013; Andersen & Hallin, 2016; Burgelman & Grove, 2007). However, Taleb, Goldstein, and Spitznagel (2009) argue that executives favor short-term profits for investments to avoid future losses and thus optimize operations, which makes adaptive processes supported by organizational slack highly vulnerable (e.g., Bromiley, 2005). So, part of the explanation for unsustainable performance outcomes may relate to an executive urge to pursue short-term profitability at the expense of longer-term resilience.

The adaptive capabilities may also be affected by executive characteristics that can change over time. For example, CEO tenure has an inverted relationship to the introduction of new inventions (Wu, Levitas, & Priem, 2005) and risk-taking behaviors that drive entrepreneurial initiatives (Simsek, 2007). Risk behavior and ethical conduct matter with firms performing above expectations display more adverse illegal executive activities (e.g., Harris & Bromiley, 2007; Jennings, 2006; Mishina, Dykes, Block, & Pollock, 2010). Psychological factors such as humbleness, optimism, and overconfidence can have adverse effects on executive risk preferences (e.g., Brenner, 2014; Ou, Seo, Choi, & Hom, 2017; Ou, Tsui, Kinicki, Waldman, Xiao, & Song, 2014; Schrand & Zechman, 2012; Shefrin, 2016a, 2016b). Hence, a comparative case study finds that organizational transition from high performance to failure *begins with dysfunctional leadership and ineffective corporate governance* (Heracleous & Werres, 2016, p. 491).

In short, the negative performance tails and inverse risk-return dynamic are influenced by executive behaviors and longer-term effects from the ability to adapt to disruptive changes imposed by extreme events in the global environment. So, we need to go behind the performance data and uncover the true nature of these intermediate and longer-term dynamics to understand the adaptive processes that lead to the observed risk-return relationships with few high performers and many extreme negative performers across different industries.

Methodological Approach

While the rationales derived from the literature can develop propositions that address the implied how, what, and why questions (e.g., Whetten, 1989) there is not a comprehensive theory to explain how the observed performance phenomena come about. Maybe there is a need for insights from multiple theories to reach at satisfactory explanations for the complex phenomena. To set in motion the task of uncovering such insights, the ensuing chapters describe how we extract a comprehensive dataset to test and further explore the implied performance characteristics and risk-return relationships based on updated information. However, given the shortcomings of conventional normality-based statistical techniques, we find a complementing case study approach relevant (Yin, 2013), which we apply in more detailed studies of outlier firms using a forensic information collection approach. Adopting multiple case studies allows for comparative and contrastive analyses (Eisenhardt, 1989, 1991) between underperforming and over-performing firms located in the tails of the performance distribution. We consider data over the extended 25-year sampling period applying a mixture of retrospective and contemporaneous information from multiple sources to enhance the internal validity of findings (Leonard-Barton, 1990). Adopting more qualitative studies to complement the analyses can help us uncover important circumstances that generate new insights (Bettis, Gambardella, Helfat, & Mitchell, 2015).

The eventual examination of the outlier firms is preceded by a review of the related strategic adaptation literature to provide a *framing logic* (Bettis et al., 2015, p. 637) combined with quantitative analyses of the collected dataset to guide the search for insights. In some ways this represents an abductive learning process that can help reassessment of prior and current observations (Dougherty, 2016) and inspire new ideas to update existing theories (Siggelkow, 2007). In support of the empirical analyses, we extracted annual performance data over the previous 25 years from the Compustat database. The collected data cover periodic economic scenarios linked to financial crisis, market adjustments, and shifts in industry structure that constitute major environmental changes the sampled firms would have to deal with.

The events that affect the observed firm performance outcomes appear to change in frequency and intensity counting the impacts from financial crisis, military conflict, cybercrime, climate change, and extreme weather events (World Economic Forum, 2022). Some of these causes derive from systemic socioeconomic mechanisms, destructive behaviors, and effects of climate change beyond direct control of individual organizations and societies (e.g., Taleb & Goldstein, 2012). We also see that extreme events often are international in scope with reinforcing global systemic effects (Smith & Fischbacher, 2009). Yet, we note that some organizations are able to deal with adversity and thrive on changing conditions, which can inspire the study of effective approaches to deal with abrupt environmental changes. A resilience perspective attempts to do this by engaging available resources across networked relationships to enable effective responses and support strategic adaptation.

Resilience to Complexity

Dynamic complex systems can also lead to spontaneous innovation and creativity that may arrive at future solutions in unpredictable ways as networked individuals engage to take action and learn from their positive experiences as possible ways forward. Resilient organizations prepare for the worst and take actions when risk events emerge and come to fruition. This thrives on leadership support, engaged interaction, slack resources, and creativity to foster adaptive responses in the face of abrupt changes (Kantur & Isery-Say, 2012). It entails supportive belief, emotional stability, self-efficacy, autonomy, reflective thinking, and social behavior among engaged individuals (Abdullah, Noor, & Ibrahim, 2013). Resilience is an ability to face disruption from unexpected events and persevere (Annarelli & Nonino, 2016). This ability is influenced by inclusive decision structure, open information processing, engagement and entrepreneurial drive to reduce adversity and move toward a more desirable state by redesigning and transforming operations learning along the way (Park, Seager, Rao, Convertino, & Linkov, 2013).

Formal planning is a common approach to deal with anticipated changes attempting to prepare for them through comprehensive analyses. It requires that major events can be identified and assessed in advance to prepare timely responses. It reflects control-based balanced scorecard thinking where performance is monitored and adjusted when it diverges from the original plan. However, these approaches are less effective when faced with the so-called wicked problems girded with high uncertainty. Wicked problems reflect highly complex issues that cannot be resolved using traditional optimization techniques. Collaborative approaches engaging multiple stakeholders with a diversity of relevant expertise and knowledge may facilitate the development of better solutions that exceed the capacity of individual decision-makers.

Organization studies consider decentralization as a proper structure to deal with dynamic environmental changes (Child & McGrath, 2001) but is insufficient on its own. It requires structural regularity that can accommodate structure and adaptive responses at the same time. It may call for combined advantages of central integration and decentralized responsiveness in line with conceptualizations of organizational actions and outcomes coming about though both planned decisions and emergent initiatives taken as the environments changes (Mintzberg & Waters, 1985). Hence, firms with successful strategic renewal capabilities seem to allocate resources both as centrally induced investments but also in the form of autonomous investments (Burgelman & Grove, 2007). The central investments support the current business model and decentralized investments focus on new business opportunities thus creating a balance between exploiting existing competencies and exploring for new ways to operate. Hence, organizations that combine central intended processes with decentralized autonomous initiatives are found to outperform their peers and display better risk-return profiles (e.g., Andersen, 2010). The dynamic adaptive systems in organizations are, therefore, arguably constituted by combinations of fast decentralized responses and slow analytical thinking at the center (Andersen & Fredens, 2013).

Interim Conclusion

The contemporary risk landscapes appear to be changing toward situations of high uncertainty and unpredictable conditions with (potentially) extreme outcome effects resembling dynamic complex business contexts that impose wicked problems on organizations that are hard for them to resolve. The conventional planning-based control approaches are ineffective in dealing with the implied non-linear and unpredictable surprises that arise from these environmental contexts. There appears to be a need for new adaptive approaches in organizations that may hone the firms' collaborative stakeholder relationships. These possibilities will be considered as the study of updated performance data progresses in the following presentations.

The Ensuing Chapters

In Chapter 2, we describe how two comprehensive corporate datasets for North America and Europe were extracted from the Compustat databases including a range of key performance variables incorporated for firms that operate across different specified industry segments. The data cleaning process is explained in detail as are alternative ways of dealing with missing values in the samples considering separate imputation techniques and complete case approaches while assessing effects on data availability and value ranges.

In Chapter 3, we make preliminary analyses of the consequences from adopting divergent imputation techniques comparing outcomes to the original untreated sample and the complete case data in terms of number firms included in the final samples and the average life span of firms. We observe distinct difference in the characteristic features of the performance distributions across the various methodologies expressed by the associated skewness and kurtosis measures. Finally, we analyze how alternative data treatments affect the number of outliers, and "extreme" outliers, in the final samples while investigating the persistency of the outlier phenomenon.

Chapter 4 extends the data analyses with a more focused examination of the outlier phenomenon as it plays out in different industry contexts to assess the consistency of the distribution characteristics uncovered in the preliminary probes. For each of the major industry sectors, we construe the frequency diagrams for a key performance variable and present them for visual examination to evaluate whether the observed outcomes relate to a few outlying observations or refer to more consistent outcome behaviors. The analyses are extended to consider the specific negative and positive outlier effects and their persistent presence in the distribution tails over extended periods of time. We further investigate the extent to which the outlier phenomenon is related to firm size using different cut-off points while assessing the relative closeness the samples show to fulfillment of the commonly assumed normality criteria.

So how can we make sense of the observed distribution characteristics and risk effects across the various samples of firm performance outcomes and get closer to explaining their prevalence in the collected empirical datasets? That is the theme of Chapter 5 where we delve into prior literatures that have been dealing with these and related issues. It is observed how conditions in the business environments that surround the activities of firms, and that expectedly will influence their performance outcomes, seem to be characterized by high levels of uncertainty and potentially extreme impacts of unexpected events. The review of empirical studies of firm performance takes its starting point in (strategic) management studies dating back to the early 1980s where steady performance outcomes are found associated with higher average performance. This implies an inverse risk-return relationship that is shown to partially derive from left-skewed outcome distributions but also implicates different time-bound relationships between performance levels and risk outcomes and vice versa. This is contrasted with empirical studies in the finance literature where we observe some commonalities in findings over time and it provides the background for additional and more detailed studies of firm performance and risk outcomes.

In Chapter 6, we present more detailed studies based on the collected performance data aimed to (re-)test earlier findings based on the new comprehensive updated datasets using the complete case samples for firms operating across various manufacturing industries as is the norm for prior empirical management studies. The analyses consider the possible links in ratio-based return measures between the numerator and denominator variables as well as their origins from reported accounting data that could be subjected to management manipulation. We apply different return measures to increase the robustness of results and also consider possible effects of leadership traits and structural aspects of the organizations assessed both across different industry contexts and business cycle intervals. The analytical results largely reproduce earlier basic findings in terms of performance distribution characteristics and risk-return relationships but we can still question the common interpretation of these general results.

Chapter 7 presents an alternative strategic responsiveness model as a possible explanation for the empirically observed performance distributions and risk outcomes that are generally found across the large sample of firms operating in different manufacturing industries. The underlying idea is that as firms address the (often) uncertain and unpredictable surroundings, they show quite different response capabilities to deal with the ongoing environmental changes, thus presenting vastly different abilities to adapt business activities to current market requirements. Assuming that good adaptation is associated with higher performance because current demands are met, we follow that it will produce more steady performance outcomes at a higher level of accomplishment over time. This adaptive model is formalized and used as the basis for computational simulations that consider different types of environmental disturbances to investigate the effects on the performance distribution and the risk-return relationships. We find that the model generates outcomes largely consistent with the observed empirical data.

As performance outliers typically are ignored in mainstream management studies, we used a standard winsorization technique to extract 23 outlying firms in the negative and positive tails of the performance distribution for further scrutiny. This is the subject of Chapter 8. We conduct comparative case studies of representative (negative and positive) outliers based on information gathered from public sources using a forensic approach as these firms were dealing with events over an extended period of time where direct personal contacts cannot be establish. The analyses identifies distinct discrepancies between under- and over-performing firms showing influence of structural aspects and managerial organizational traits where firms in the positive tail seem to display the contours of unique adaptive capabilities that sustain performance.

We round off the story line that presents different stages of a more extensive research project by providing a final overview of the progressing analyses, the cumulated findings, and some concluding remarks. So, the final chapter (Chapter 9) summarizes the different phases of the study and discusses the implications of the presented findings with some thoughts about the managerial takeaway and a promising future research focus.

Each chapter appears as a standalone contribution that can be read as an independent study as well as constitute consecutive and progressing studies to be consumed as you prefer. We hope you enjoy the reading and will find some useful insights in the process.

References

Abdullah, N. A. S., Noor, N. L. M., & Ibrahim, E. N. M. (2013). Resilient organization: Modelling the capacity for resilience. In *Research and innovation in information systems* (ICRIIS), International Conference on IEEE (pp. 319–324).

Andersen, T. J. (2010). Combining central planning and decentralization to enhance effective risk management outcomes. *Risk Management, 12*(2), 101–115.

Andersen, T. J. (2015a). Strategic adaptation. In J. D. Wright (Ed.), *International encyclopedia of the social & behavioral sciences* (pp. 501–507). Amsterdam: Elsevier Science.

Andersen, T. J. (2015b). Interactive strategy-making: Combining central reasoning with ongoing learning from decentralized responses. *Journal of General Management, 40*(4), 69–88.

Andersen, T. J., & Bettis, R. A. (2014). The risk-return outcomes of strategic responsiveness. In T. J. Andersen (Ed.), *Contemporary challenges in risk management* (pp. 63–90). London: Palgrave Macmillan.

Andersen, T. J., & Bettis, R. A. (2015). Exploring longitudinal risk-return relationships. *Strategic Management Journal, 36*(8), 1135–1145.

Andersen, T. J., Denrell, J., & Bettis, R. A. (2007). Strategic responsiveness and Bowman's risk–return paradox. *Strategic Management Journal, 28*(4), 407–429.

Andersen, T. J., & Fredens, K. (2013). *The responsive organization.* CGRS Working Paper Series No. 1. Center for Global Strategic Responsiveness, Copenhagen Business School, Copenhagen.

Andersen, T. J., & Hallin, C.A. (2016). The adaptive organization and fast-slow systems. In R. J. Aldag (Ed.), *Oxford research encyclopedias: Business and management.* Oxford: Oxford University Press.

Annarelli, A., & Nonino, F. (2016). Strategic and operational management of organizational resilience: Current state of research and future directions, *Omega, 62*, 1–18.

Baum, J. A., & McKelvey, B. (2006). *Analysis of extremes in management studies.* In D. J. Ketcehn & D. D. Bergh (Eds.), *Research methodology in strategy and management* (pp. 123–196). Bingley: Emerald Publishing.

Bettis, R. A., Gambardella, A., Helfat, C., & Mitchell, W. (2015). Qualitative empirical research in strategic management. *Strategic Management Journal, 36*, 637–639.

Bloom, N., & Van Reenen, J. (2007). Measuring and explaining management practices across firms and countries. *Quarterly Journal of Economics, 122*(4), 1351–1408.

Boisot, M., & McKelvey, B. (2011). Connectivity, extremes, and adaptation: A power-law perspective of organizational effectiveness. *Journal of Management Inquiry, 20*(2), 119–133.

Bower, J. L., & Gilbert, C. G. (Eds.). (2005). *From resource allocation to strategy.* New York, NY: Oxford University Press.

Bowman, E. H. (1980). *A risk/return paradox for strategic management.* Working paper No. WP 1107-80. Alfred P. Sloan School of Management, Massachusetts Institute of Technology (MIT), Cambridge, MA.

Brenner, S. (2014). The risk preferences of US executives. *Management Science, 61*(6), 1344–1361.

Bromiley, P. (1991a). Testing a causal model of corporate risk taking and performance. *Academy of Management Journal, 34*(1), 37–59.

Bromiley, P. (1991b). Paradox or at least variance found: A comment on "Mean-variance approaches to risk–return relationships in strategy: Paradox lost". *Management Science, 37*(9), 1206–1210.

Bromiley, P. (2005). *The behavioral foundations of strategic management*. Hoboken, NJ: Blackwell Publishing.

Burgelman, R. A. (1983). A process model of internal corporate venturing in the diversified major firm. *Administrative Science Quarterly, 28*(2), 223–244.

Burgelman, R. A. (1996). A process model of strategic business exit: Implications for an evolutionary perspective on strategy. *Strategic Management Journal, 17*(S1), 193–214.

Burgelman, R. A., & Grove, A. S. (2007). Let chaos reign, then rein in chaos—Repeatedly: Managing strategic dynamics for corporate longevity. *Strategic Management Journal, 28*(10), 965–979.

Child, J., & McGrath, R. G. (2001). Organizations unfettered: Organizational form in an information-intensive economy. *Academy of Management Journal, 44*(6), 1135–1148.

Dougherty, D. J. (2016). *Taking advantage of emergence: Productively innovating in complex innovation systems*. Oxford: Oxford University Press.

Eisenhardt, K. M. (1989). Building theories from case study research. *Academy of Management Review, 14*(4), 532–550.

Eisenhardt, K. M. (1991). Better stories and better constructs: The case for rigor and comparative logic. *Academy of Management Review, 16*(3), 620–627.

Harris, J., & Bromiley, P. (2007). Incentives to cheat: The influence of executive compensation and firm performance on financial misrepresentation. *Organization Science, 18*(3), 350–367.

Helfat, C. E. (2007). Stylized facts, empirical research and theory development in management. *Strategic Organization, 5*(2), 185–192.

Henkel, J. (2009). The risk-return paradox for strategic management: Disentangling true and spurious effects. *Strategic Management Journal, 30*(3), 287–303.

Heracleous, L., & Werres, K. (2016). On the road to disaster: Strategic misalignments and corporate failure. *Long Range Planning, 49*(4), 491–506.

Jennings, M. M. (2006). *The seven signs of ethical collapse*. New York, NY: St. Martins Press.

Kantur, D., & Isery-Say, A. (2012). Organizational resilience: A conceptual integrative framework. *Journal of Management & Organization, 18*(6), 762–773.

Leonard-Barton, D. (1990). A dual methodology for case studies: Synergistic use of a longitudinal single site with replicated multiple sites. *Organization Science, 1*(3), 248–266.

Mishina, Y., Dykes, B. J., Block, E. S., & Pollock, T. G. (2010). Why "good" firms do bad things: The effects of high aspirations, high expectations, and prominence on the incidence of corporate illegality. *Academy of Management Journal, 53*(4), 701–722.

Mintzberg, H., & Waters, J. A. (1985). Of strategies deliberate and emergent. *Strategic Management Journal, 6*, 257–272.

Ou, A. Y., Seo, J. J., Choi, D., & Hom, P. (2017). When can humble top executives retain middle managers? The moderating role of top management team faultlines. *Academy of Management Journal, 60*(5), 1915–1931.

Ou, A. Y., Tsui, A. S., Kinicki, A. J., Waldman, D. A., Xiao, Z., & Song, L. J. (2014). Humble chief executive officers' connections to top management team integration and middle managers' responses. *Administrative Science Quarterly, 59*(1), 34–72.

Park, J., Seager, T. P., Rao, P. S. C., Convertino, M., & Linkov, I. (2013). Integrating risk and resilience approaches to catastrophe management in engineering systems. *Risk Analysis, 33*(3), 356–367.

Schrand, C. M., & Zechman, S. L. (2012). Executive overconfidence and the slippery slope to financial misreporting. *Journal of Accounting and Economics, 53*(1), 311–329.

Sharpe, W. F. (1964). Capital asset prices: A theory of market equilibrium under conditions of risk. *The Journal of Finance, 19*(3), 425–442.

Shefrin, H. (2016a). *Behavioral risk management.* London: Palgrave Macmillan.

Shefrin, H. (2016b). How psychological pitfalls generated the global financial crisis. In T. J. Andersen (Ed.), *The Routledge companion to strategic risk management* (pp. 269–295). Abingdon: Routledge.

Siggelkow, N. (2007). Persuasion with case studies. *Academy of Management Journal, 50*(1), 20–24.

Silber, I., Israeli, Bustin, A., & Zvi, O. B. (2009). Recovery strategies for service failures: The case of restaurants. *Journal of Hospitality Marketing & Management, 18*, 730–740.

Simsek, Z. (2007). CEO tenure and organizational performance: An intervening model. *Strategic Management Journal, 28*(6), 653–662.

Smith, D., & Fischbacher, M. (2009). The changing nature of risk management: The challenge of borders, uncertainty and resilience. *Risk Management, 11*, 1–12.

Taleb, N. N. (2007). *The Black Swan: The impact of the highly improbable.* New York, NY: Random House.

Taleb, N. N., & Goldstein, D. G. (2012). The problem is beyond psychology: The real world is more random than regression analyses. *International Journal of Forecasting, 28*(3), 715–716.

Taleb, N. N., Goldstein, D. G., & Spitznagel, M. W. (2009). The six mistakes executives make in risk management. *Harvard Business Review, 87*(10), 78–81.

Van der Vegt, G. S., Essens, P., Wahlström, M., & George, G. (2015). Managing risk and resilience. *Academy of Management Journal, 58*(4), 971–980.

Whetten, D. A. (1989). What constitutes a theoretical contribution? *Academy of Management Review, 14*(4), 490–495.

Wu, S., Levitas, E., & Priem, R. L. (2005). CEO tenure and company invention under differing levels of technological dynamism. *Academy of Management Journal, 48*(5), 859–873.

World Economic Forum. (2022). *The Global Risk Report 2022 – Insight report* (17th ed.). Geneva: The Global Competitiveness and Risk Team, World Economic Forum.

Yin, R. K. (2013). *Case study research: Design and methods.* Thousand Oaks, CA: Sage Publications.

Chapter 2

Collecting the Data*

Abstract

This chapter outlines how the comprehensive North American and European datasets were collected and explains the ensuing data cleaning process outlining three alternative methods applied to deal with missing values, the complete case, the multiple imputation (MI), and the K-nearest neighbor (KNN) methods. The complete case method is the conventional approach adopted in many mainstream management studies. We further discuss the implied assumption underlying use of this technique, which is rarely assessed, or tested in practice and explain the alternative imputation approaches in detail. Use of North American data is the norm but we also collected a European dataset, which is rarely done to enable subsequent comparative analysis between these geographical regions. We introduce the structure of firms organized within different industry classification schemes for use in the ensuing comparative analyses and provide base information on missing values in the original and cleaned datasets. The calculated performance indicators derived from the sampled data are defined and presented. We show how the three alternative approaches considered to deal with missing values have significantly different effects on the calculated performance measures in terms of extreme estimate ranges and mean performance values.

Keywords: Complete case method; data cleaning; K-nearest neighbor method; missing values; multiple imputation method; performance measures

---

*As research assistant engaged in the project, Martin Albæk was instrumental in collecting and treating the datasets presented and applied in the ensuing analysis.

A Study of Risky Business Outcomes: Adapting to Strategic Disruption, 15–28
Copyright © 2023 by Torben Juul Andersen
Published under exclusive licence by Emerald Publishing Limited
doi:10.1108/978-1-83797-074-220231002

Introduction

To enable an investigation of prevalent performance distributions and risk-return relationships, we decided to create a comprehensive database of firms located in major developed economies across North America as well as Europe. A majority of prior studies adopt North American data because they historically have been more established and accessible. However, European datasets are improving and, therefore, we consider them in the preliminary data studies to investigate whether European firms generally display performance patterns that are comparable to North American firms, or if we discern noticeable differences.

We extracted performance data for all firms included on the Standard & Poors Compustat North American and Compustat Global databases for an extensive updated 25-year period from 1995 to 2019. Hence, the data collection ended just before the first economic effects related to COVID-19 were observed from 2020 onwards. The first dataset includes publicly listed companies traded on various stock exchanges in the USA and Canada, whereas the second dataset includes information on international companies based outside of North America.[1] The decision to consider a longer time period was made to enable assessment of performance outcomes across different subperiods where business conditions and economic growth differ and thereby uncover potential effects of varied environmental states. This was done as a means to gain insights across business cycles and increase the robustness of analytical results. The data collection focused solely on firms with at least five years of consecutive annual performance data recorded in the databases to enable meaningful calculation of performance variance (standard deviation in returns) commonly used as an indicator of performance risk.

The two Compustat databases are developed and managed by Standard & Poor's (S&P), the American credit rating and financial research agency. S&P on its end collects the data from official filings with regulatory agencies, annual and interim reports, company and exchange websites, and various public news and press releases. The North American databases have been the most common sources for academic studies, so we decided to additionally extract data from a subset of European countries to compare the characteristics of the North American data with the European data, which is only rarely done, if at all. More specifically, we included firm data from countries belonging to the European Economic Area (EEA), plus Switzerland. This was done because these countries are considered to comprise economies with developed market structures and institutions that are comparable to those observed in Canada and the USA. This provides a stronger basis for comparative analysis and validation of outcomes obtained from the two datasets.

With respect to the North American data, we specifically retrieved them from the Compustat North American Fundamental Annuals database. The European data on income statements and various balance sheet items were retrieved from

---

[1]As a consequence a (smaller) subset of multinational firms headquartered in different parts of the world with their equity listed on stock exchanges in North America are part of this dataset.

the Compustat Global Fundamentals Annuals consolidated database, whereas data on company stock prices and number of shares outstanding were extracted from the Compustat Global Security Daily dataset. Finally, annual inflation and exchange rates were retrieved from the Organization for Economic and Co-operation and Development (OECD), a transnational organization aimed at increasing economic cooperation among developed economies proposing guidelines for joint policy-making. These data were used to convert all the annual data over the period 1996–2019 into 1995 values as a comparable reference.

Since business sectors and industry contexts vary in structural and dynamic components reflecting diverse competitive and performance trajectories (e.g., Porter, 1980, 2008), the firm data were organized in accordance with common industry classification scheme, thus allowing us to generate comprehensive cross-sectional data samples with clearly defined industry subsamples. Since industry definitions can be difficult to determine with precision, we organized the corporate data in accordance with two alternative industry classification schemes, the Standard Industrial Classification (SIC) division, created by the US Government, and the Securities and Exchange Commission Office (SEC) classification, retrieved from the official website of the US Securities and Exchange Commission. This allowed us to analyze the economic activity level and firm responses in these specified industry contexts. We use both classifications in the ensuing analyses.

Constructing the Dataset

We collected data from all types of companies across industries but excluded banks and other deposit-taking institutions from the data samples because these specialized organizations operate in highly regulated industries and are expected to behave differently from firms engaged in various forms of production and services. We assembled additional information on balance sheet items to construe basic performance measures and return ratios including total assets (AT), total liabilities (LT), current liabilities (LCT), total revenues ($REVT$), operating activities net cash flows ($OANCF$), operating income before depreciation ($OIBDP$), and net income (NI). The firms' market capitalization ($MKTCAP$) is readily available for firms included in the North American dataset whereas that is not the case for the European dataset. To obtain this information, we downloaded data from the Compustat Global security daily to construe the market-based return measure, Tobin's q (TQ). We multiplied the closing price ($PRCCF$) reported at the last day each year by the number of outstanding common shares ($CSHO$) to calculate the market capitalization.

The key performance variables used in the ensuing analysis were determined as follows:

$$ROA = \frac{NI}{AT}$$

$$OPM = \frac{OIBDP}{REVT}$$

$$CEQ = AT - LT$$

$$CFRE = \frac{OANCF}{AT}$$

$$CE = AT - LCT$$

$$TQ = \frac{MKTCAP + AT - CEQ}{AT}$$

where NI = net income
$OIBDP$ = operating income before depreciation
$OANCF$ = operating activities net cash flows
AT = total assets
LT = total liabilities
LCT = current liabilities
CEQ = equity book value
CE = capital employed
$REVT$ = total revenues
ROA = return on assets
OPM = operating margin
$CFRE$ = cash flow return
TQ = Tobin's q

The two datasets for North America and Europe include firms that operate across all industry segments (excluding banks and other deposit-taking institutions) to allow comparative analyses between the full cross-sectional sample and across different industry subsamples. The following accounts for the different industry segments following the Securities and Exchange Commission Office (SEC) classification and the SIC. For an overview, please refer to Table 2.1 (Panels A and B).

Cleaning the Data

We wanted to use the performance data to analyze if there appears to be persistent under- or over-performers among the sampled firms by looking at the distribution of the various performance measures outlined and described above. To assess this properly, we must apply representative datasets of some size with a sufficiently high number of observations to ensure statistical power. To achieve this, we applied the principle of making as few modifications to the raw data as possible to retain the largest possible number of firms in the total sample while considering different imputation techniques to generate sensible datapoint for replacement of missing values. The data cleaning and imputation methods are based on applications of the free software environment R for statistical computing and graphics (The R foundation, 2020).

Table 2.1.   The Industry Classification Systems.

Panel A: SEC—Office Filing Classification

SEC Office	SIC four-digit codes belonging to the SEC Office
Life Science	100–900, 2800–2891, 3821–3873, 8000–8093
Energy & Transportation	1000–1400, 2911–2990, 4011–4731, 4900–4991
Real Estate & Construction	1520–1731, 6500–7011, 9995
Manufacturing	2000–2790, 3011–3490, 3600–3812, 3910–3990
Technology	3510–3590, 4812–4899, 7370–7374
Trade & Services	5000–5990, 7200–7363, 7377–7997, 8111–8744, 8900
Finance (excl. banks: 6000-6099)	6111–6411
International Corporations	8880–8889, 9721

Panel B: Standard Industrial Classification

SIC Division	SIC four-digit codes belonging to the SIC Division
Agriculture, Forestry, Fishing	0000–999
Mining and Construction	1000–1999
Manufacturing (food, apparel, furniture, pharmaceuticals)[a]	2000–2999
Manufacturing (materials, machines, equipment, computers)[b]	3000–3999
Transportation, Communication, and Distribution	4000–4999
Wholesale and Retail	5000–5999
Finance, Insurance, and Real estate (excl. banks: 6000–6099)	6000–6999
Other	7000–9999

[a] Medicinal chemicals (2833), Pharmaceuticals (2834), Diagnostic substances (2835), Biological products (2836).

[b] Computer technologies (3570, 3571, 3572, 3575, 3576), Electronics components and Semiconductors (3670, 3672, 3674, 3677, 3678, 3679).

The data cleaning process attempts to detect and correct for inaccuracies observed in the data as uncovered from the raw untreated datasets. Most of this effort, although not all of it, constitute attempts to deal effectively with the issue of missing values. It is necessary to consider the prevalence of missing values in the dataset to enable ensuing data analyses where most statistical software is unable to interpret the missing data points. To assess possibility for missing value effects, we first needed to understand how some of the data points turned into missing values to devise proper ways of replacing them. The North American dataset has a longer track record with substantially more firms included but also has a much higher relative share of missing values (18.3% against 4.3%) compared to the European dataset (Table 2.2).

The North American dataset has almost three times the number of recorded value points, observed variables, and collected individual firms compared to the European dataset (Table 2.2). However, the European dataset has a much lower share of missing values. More importantly, the comparative statistics of the two datasets illustrate how the choice of different definitions, or descriptions of the missing values influence our interpretation of how much data are missing. For instance, if we focus on the share of missing values, the North American and European datasets represent less than 20% and 5% of missing values, respectively. However, if we focus on the share of firms with missing value in the collected samples, we see that around 75% of firms in the North American sample and almost 50% in the European dataset have missing values.

As we examine the registered data, we can also observe that some firms have negative values posted for *AT*, *LT*, *LCT*, and *REVT*, which obviously should not be possible and thus must derive from errors. It suggests that this information has been wrongly collected, or recorded by mistake, and therefore we should change those data points to missing values. For some reason a number of firms have the same financial year presented twice in the datasets. In these instances of double

Table 2.2. Summary of Missing Values in the Original Datasets.

	Geographical Region	
	North America	**Europe**
Recorded value points	4,898,907	1,877,055
Observed variables	288,171	110,415
Number of individual firms	30,776	10,716
Share of missing values[a]	18.29%	4.31%
Share of variables with missing values[b]	40.58%	18.40%
Share of firms with missing values[c]	74.18%	46.45%

Note: This table is construed by analyzing missing data in a subset of the full dataset including all the variables, *at, lt, lct, revt, oancf, oibdp, ni, mktcap, prccf, roa, opm, ceq, cfre, ce, tq*.
[a] Calculated on the basis of the recorded data points.
[b] Calculated on the basis of the observed variables.
[c] Calculated on the basis of the number of firms.

count, we drop the subsequent annual observations and retain the first year of reported data. Furthermore, we also find some negative values on the computed variables *CEQ*, *CE*, and *TQ*, which contravenes the accounting rules for a going concern. Hence, it is not possible to maintain these records in the dataset and we must convert them to missing values as well.

Based on these adjusted data records, we applied three different approaches of dealing with missing values considering whether or not to apply (two alternative) imputation techniques to generate reasonable numerical replacements for missing data to create a more complete dataset, or deleting all the firms with less than complete datasets from the sample. The way the missing data points are distributed across the sample will have an influence on how the final datasets are construed. The three methods considered in the following include the so-called Complete Case approach (where the dataset is reduced by all firms that have observations with missing data) and two different imputation techniques, the Multiple Imputation Chained Equation (MICE) and the KNN mean approaches. These methodological approaches are explained in further detail in the following sections.

Complete Case Approach

The complete case approach drops any company that has a missing value in one of the variables used for the analysis over the sampled time period. This technique is the most commonly adopted approach to deal with the issue of missing values in empirical finance and management studies. However, this methodology should only be adopted when it is reasonable to assume that the missing values derive from completely random causes (Wooldridge, 2010). That is, if the missing data values arise independently of type of variable, or type of observation, the remaining values in that dataset can be assumed to represent the population, otherwise not. This is a fairly strong assumption but also one that typically is not taken into consideration when deciding whether the complete case approach is to be adopted. The truth is that the underlying assumptions often may fail to hold, particularly in the case of longitudinal panel data such as those collected here for our analytical purposes (Hair, Black, Babin, & Anderson, 2010). Hence, the data may hold information formed by consistent changes and development paths of individual firms reflected in the time-stamped data points included in the collected value strings. In these cases, it is appropriate to consider applications of the proposed MICE and KNN mean imputation techniques to capture systematic data relationships as criteria for replacing the missing data points with meaningful values. We compare the two approaches and base our conclusions on the imputed datasets generated by the two techniques adopted to circumvent possible effects of simplifying assumptions about data missing-completely-at-random (MCAR). It is interesting to also analyze the complete case approach, where firms with missing values are deleted from the final sample. Since this is the common approach to deal with missing values, it is highly relevant to compare the results from the imputed datasets with outcomes derived from this conventional method.

Adopting the complete case approach on the modified sample causes the North American dataset to drop about 69% of the sampled firms corresponding to around 68% of all the recorded observations, that is, a substantial part of the collected data are lost. In the European dataset, the complete case approach drops 56% of the firms and 64% of all observations. We notice that the complete case approach eliminates, or drops the most extreme values recorded in the databases (see Appendix 2.1). Looking at return on assets (ROA), the min/max range is reduced (−49.9%/1.4% vs. −15.6%/1.3%) in the North American dataset (Panels A and B) and (−4.1%/0.5% vs. −3.6%/0.5%) in the European dataset (Panels C and D). As a consequence, the mean value of ROA converge toward zero, that is, increasing from −0.098% to 0.005% in the North American dataset and from −0.031% to −0.005% in the European dataset (Appendix 2.1).

The firms that post the most extreme values are also those with the least number of available complete data. This is further captured by the fact that the minimum and maximum values for most of the performance measures change and converge toward lower differentials when we adopt the complete case approach (Appendix 2.1). This suggests that there is some relationship between the missing values and other recorded values, which contravenes the strong MCAR assumption and speaks against adopting the complete case approach. A rule of thumb for using the complete case approach is to apply it when there is less than 5% of missing data (Graham, 2009). This is obviously far from what we observe in the two datasets collected on North American and European firms.

A more precise estimation-based assessment of MCAR conditions may adopt Little's (1988) test on each of the two datasets. The null hypothesis of this test is that the data are not MCAR, which is rejected in both our datasets. From this, adoption of the complete case approach arguably cannot be justified, or recommended as an appropriate approach of dealing with the missing values, unless it can be combined with other approaches. Hence, we adopted two alternative imputation techniques, the MI and KNN mean imputation methods, to generate values for the missing data points. These approaches are explained in the following.

Multiple Imputation Approach

When adopting imputation techniques to replace the missing data, a single imputation is often considered sufficient. It is a simpler process but does not account for potential uncertainty generated around the imputed values. That is, once the imputation is completed, the analyses proceeds as if the initially imputed values are true even though that might not really be the case. By adopting a MI approach excessive uncertainty around the imputed "true" values can be avoided by conducting multiple sequential imputation runs (Azur, Stuart, Frangakis, & Leaf, 2011). Therefore, we adopted this approach as one of the techniques to impute values for the missing data. Several MI techniques are available where we decided to use MI that incorporates chained imputation equations (MICE). The MICE algorithm assumes that the pattern of missing data is completely random as a fundamental premise. This implies that the factors, or mechanisms causing the data to be missing are independent from the data itself, which resolves issues with the data not fulfilling the MCAR assumption (Jakobsen, Gluud, Wetterslev, & Winkel, 2017). Subsequent diagnostic analyses of graphical presentations of the missing data patterns allow us to assess the data randomness and convince ourselves that we are in fact incorporating unbiased random values. The MICE procedure runs a series of regression models, where each variable with missing data is modeled based on the observed relationships to all the other variables that are included in the dataset. Each of the variables is then modeled, predicted, and selected in accordance with its own assumed distribution (White, Daniel, & Royston, 2010).

The MICE algorithm was coded to create five complete datasets, by running 20 iterations using a predictive mean matching (PMM) technique to impute the missing values. That is, for each missing observation, the algorithm selects a set of candidate donor values from other complete observations that are close to the predicted value for the missing data point. The value is then drawn at random from these available donor candidates to replace the missing value, assuming that the missing value follows the same distribution (Buuren, 2018).

To inspect for potential convergence issues, the estimated values were plotted against the number of specified iterations in the so-called "trace plots" where convergence is present when the variance between different sequences is no larger than the variance between individual sequences. The algorithm was specified so that the values for missing data fulfill all the basic accounting principles as specified earlier for all the performance measures and return ratios we are using (Buuren & Groothuis-Oudshoorn, 2011) thereby upholding the validity of the imputed values.

KNN Approach

By adopting the KNN methodology, the algorithm follows a "closest fit" (CF) technique (Grzymala-Busse, 2005; Kaiser, 2014) by looking at the number of k "closest" observations to the missing value. More specifically, the CF technique replaces the missing values with an existing value of the same variable from across a range of other observations choosing the one that looks most similar to the observation with missing values. The proximity is calculated by the Manhattan distance between all the variables. That is, the weighted difference between the non-missing variables belonging to the observation of interest and the variables from the observations with the non-missing values.[2] The difference between the

---

[2] Manhattan distance between x and y:

$$\text{distance}(x, y) = \sum_{i=1}^{n} \text{distance}(x_i, y_i)$$

where,

$$\text{distance}(x_i, y_i) = \begin{cases} 0 \text{ if } x_i = y_i \\ 1 \text{ if } x \text{ and } y \text{ are symbolic and } x_i \neq y_i \ \ or \ \ x_i = \text{NA} \text{ or } y_i = \text{NA} \\ \dfrac{|x_i - y_i|}{r} \text{ if } x_i \text{ and } y_i \text{ are numbers and } x_i \neq y_i \end{cases}$$

r = difference between maximum and minimum of known value
NA = missing value
i = number of observed data points $(1, \ldots, n)$

CF and the KNN approaches is that the CF method only imputes the closest observation to the missing value, where KNN looks for the k closest observations and replaces the missing value with the average of the k closest observations. To determine an appropriate value of k (number of close observations), we followed a commonly used calculative approach, or rule of thumb (Hassan et al., 2019).

$$k = \sqrt{\frac{N}{2}}$$

where,
N = total number of observations in the dataset.

The k-number (k) is then rounded down to the nearest full values, if not an integer. The k determined in relation to the North American dataset is equal to 286, whereas the k determined on the basis of the European dataset amounts to 217.

Further Data Cleaning for Smooth Imputation

To ensure the MICE algorithm will run properly, we retained firms with most values reported in the datasets thus specifically deleting companies with more than 50% of missing values in at least one of the reported years. Some of the reported data points might not represent "true" data, or constitute representative values of firm performance. To address this potential problem, we sorted the dataset for each of the performance variables, *ROA, OPM, CE, CFRE*, and *CEQ* and converted the highest and lowest 0.25% of the observations into missing values before reapplying the 50% missing value criteria. We chose these (low) marginal percentage observations as representative of very extreme data points that may be interpreted as caused by human reporting mistakes, or highly unusual circumstances, that fail to present ordinary phenomena, or observations from reality. Following this procedure, the North American dataset was reduced by 43% of its observations and 49% of its firm whereas the European dataset lost 14% of its observations and 13% of its companies. These differences are explained by the fact that the North American dataset has a higher number of firms with missing values whereas the European dataset appears to have the majority of missing values concentrated across a smaller number of firms.

The effect of this data manipulation performed on each of the two datasets can be observed by how the share of missing values and observations with missing values drops in the North American dataset and slightly increases in the European dataset, as the most extreme values of the performance ratios were substituted with missing values (Table 2.3).

For consistency and ease of comparison to the MICE methodology, the KNN mean approach was applied on the same adapted dataset as used for the MICE imputation. We performed more detailed analyses of the deleted observations and firms in the sample to ascertain the correctness of their exclusion from the sample. The following provides two examples to illustrate the implied analysis including one example from each of the two datasets.

Table 2.3. Summary of Missing Values After Cleaning the Datasets.

	Geographical Region	
	North America	**Europe**
Recorder value points	2,781,455	1,607,724
Observed variables	163,615	94,572
Number of individual firms	15,519	9,288
Share of missing values[a]	6.16%	5.94%
Share of variables with missing values[b]	31.15%	21.83%
Share of firms with missing values[c]	69.08%	55.68%

Note: The table is construed by analyzing missing data in a subset of the full dataset including the variables *at, lt, lct, revt, oancf, oibdp, ni, mktcap, prccf, roa, opm, ceq, cfre, ce, tq*.
[a] Calculated on the basis of the recorded value points.
[b] Calculated on the basis of the observed variables.
[c] Calculated on the basis of the number of firms.

Starting with the North American dataset, one of the firms with observations showing extreme values is Point of Care Nano-Technology Inc. (PCNT), a company engaged in the development and patenting of a nanotechnology-based business innovation platform. Compustat reported a cash flow return for this company of −259,700%, explained by it having almost no assets while spending a lot of cash on the development of future patents with an expectation of later rewards. Although we could confirm the correctness of the data by looking at other sources, it can be assumed that such an extreme value will jeopardize the imputation technique and hence subsequent analyses. Therefore, it was considered reasonable to drop this value from the dataset and transform it into a missing value. Moreover, this company had more than 50% of missing values and was eventually dropped from the dataset in line with the principles explained before.

Turning to the European dataset, we identified an Italian firm, Italiaonline s.p.a., which according to Bloomberg records is a company developing and offering web-based marketing and digital advertising solutions. The firm recorded extreme values, which suggests that the data points are inaccurate. For instance, it presented a Tobin's q of 10,061 which is an extremely high value compared to the average value across this calculated performance variable. Looking in more detail into the data recorded on the Compustat database, we note that the share price is reported at €85 at the end of 2014, which implies a total market capitalization of €5 billion given their 64,264,615 shares outstanding. Conversely, the 2014 annual report filing of Italiaonline s.p.a. reports that the market capitalization of the company in 2014 on average amounted to €196 million. These discrepancies suggest that the stock price reported in Compustat is wrong, which thereby illustrates and provides justification for the principle of converting the 0.5% extreme values reported on each variable into missing values.

Finally, in those cases where the MICE and KNN imputations yield "impossible" accounting values, such as, negative book value of equity, capital employed, or Tobin's q, then these firms were dropped from the imputed datasets as well.

The three datasets, generated for each of the two geographical regions, based on the Complete Case, MICE, and KNN mean approaches were used as the basis for comparative analyses, that are presented in the next chapter.

References

Azur, M. J., Stuart, E. A., Frangakis, C., & Leaf, P. J. (2011). Multiple imputation by chained equations: What is it and how does it work? *International Journal of Methods in Psychiatric Research, 20*(1), 40–49.

Bloomberg. Retrieved from https://www.bloomberg.com/profile/company/PG:IM#xj4y7vzkg

Buuren, S. v. (2018). Predictive mean matching. In N. Keiding, B. J. T. Morgan, C. K. Wikle & P. van der Heijden (Eds.), *Flexible imputation of missing data* (2nd ed.). London: Chapman and Hall/CRC.

Buuren, S. v., & Groothuis-Oudshoorn, K. (2011). MICE: Multivariate imputation by chained equations in R. *Journal of Statistical Software, 45*(3), 1–67.

Graham, J. W. (2009). Missing data analysis: Making it work in the real world. *Annual Review of Psychology, 60*, 549–576.

Grzymala-Busse, W. J. (2005). Rough set strategies to data with missing attribute values. In *Foundations and novel approaches in data mining* (pp. 197–212). Berlin: Springer.

Hair, J., Black, W. C., Babin, B. J., & Anderson, R. E. (2010). *Multivariate data analysis* (7th ed.). Upper Saddle River, NJ: Pearson Education International.

Hassan, D., Rodan, A., Salem, M., & Mohammad, M. (2019). Comparative study of using data mining techniques for bank telemarketing data. *Sixth HCT information technology trends (ITT)*, November (pp. 177–181).

Jakobsen, J. C., Gluud, C., Wetterslev, J., & Winkel, P. (2017). When and how should multiple imputation be used for handling missing data in randomised clinical trials – A practical guide with flowcharts. *BMC Medical Research Methodology, 17*(1), (162–171).

Little, R. J. A. (1988). A test of missing completely at random for multivariate data with missing values. *Journal of the American Statistical Association, 83*(404), 1198–1202.

Kaiser, J. (2014). Dealing with missing values in data. *Journal of Systems Integration, 5*(1), 1804–2724.

Porter, M. E. (1980). *Competitive strategy*. New York, NY: Free Press.

Porter, M. E. (2008). The five competitive forces that shape strategy. *Harvard Business Review, 86*(1), 78–137.

The R Foundation. (2020). *R: A language and environment for statistical computing*. Vienna: R Foundation for Statistical Computing. Retrieved from http://www.r-project.org/index.html

White, I. R., Daniel, R., & Royston, P. (2010). Avoiding bias due to perfect prediction in multiple imputation of incomplete categorical variables. *Computational Statistics & Data Analysis, 54*(10), 2267–2275.

Wooldridge, J. M. (2010). *Econometric analysis of cross section and panel data* (2nd ed.). Cambridge, MA: MIT Press.

Appendix 2.1.   Distribution of Performance Measures for the European and North American Datasets (Comparing Original Data With the Complete Case Dataset)

Panel A: North America Original Data

	Obs. (1)	Companies (2)	Min. (3)	1st Qu. (4)	Mean (5)	Median (6)	3rd Qu. (7)	Max. (8)
mktCAP	163,615	15,519	0.0009	28.925	2,680.769	165.638	968.265	1,547,896.024
ROA	163,615	15,519	−49.874	−0.056	−0.098	0.021	0.064	1.423
OPM	163,615	15,519	−275.286	0.028	−0.864	0.114	0.229	0.956
CE	163,615	15,519	0.031	22.558	1,668.359	131.931	811.706	66,499.38
CFRE	163,615	15,519	−13.083	−0.01	−0.002	0.059	0.115	0.683
CEQ	163,615	15,519	0.025	19.808	996.576	98.675	501.997	4,8310.31
TQ	163,615	15,519	0.29	1.027	2.284	1.371	2.158	391.632

Panel B: North America Complete Case Dataset

	Obs. (1)	Companies (2)	Min. (3)	1st Qu. (4)	Mean (5)	Median (6)	3rd Qu. (7)	Max. (8)
mktCAP	51,704	4,798	0.0009	38.294	2,531.796	221.179	1,342.96	406,273.432
ROA	51,704	4,798	−15.64	−0.003	0.005	0.039	0.079	1.328
OPM	51,704	4,798	−231.928	0.05	−0.1	0.115	0.2	0.951
CE	51,704	4,798	0.033	32.986	1,849.181	176.621	1,035.65	65,569.58
CFRE	51,704	4,798	−13.083	0.031	0.067	0.081	0.132	0.678
CEQ	51,704	4,798	0.026	25.067	971.1	120.943	593.285	46,456.74
TQ	51,704	4,798	0.294	1.06	1.836	1.385	2.012	168.229

(Continued)

Appendix 2.1.   *(Continued)*

Panel C: Europe Original Data

	Obs. (1)	Companies (2)	Min. (3)	1st Qu. (4)	Mean (5)	Median (6)	3rd Qu. (7)	Max. (8)
mktCAP	94,572	9,288	0.0006	16.947	16,90.822	71.094	368.379	1,794,847
ROA	94,572	9,288	−4.124	−0.029	−0.031	0.028	0.066	0.487
OPM	94,572	9,288	−177	−0.025	−0.689	0.029	0.073	3.655
CE	94,572	9,288	0.085	17.513	995.35	69.753	342.679	65,993.5
CFRE	94,572	9,288	−2.2	0.004	0.035	0.066	0.118	0.534
CEQ	94,572	9,288	0.019	13.378	513.844	49.348	210.453	29,943.48
TQ	94,572	9,288	0.237	0.956	1.804	1.242	1.83	37.81

Panel D: Europe Complete Case Dataset

	Obs. (1)	Companies (2)	Min. (3)	1st Qu. (4)	Mean (5)	Median (6)	3rd Qu. (7)	Max. (8)
mktCAP	34,513	4,116	0.037	17.95	809.932	65.272	293.367	256,394.7
ROA	34,513	4,116	−3.591	−0.011	−0.005	0.034	0.074	0.481
OPM	34,513	4,116	−170.364	−0.012	−0.365	0.033	0.078	3.453
CE	34,513	4,116	0.09	15.799	586.094	52.946	218.833	48,484.602
CFRE	34,513	4,116	−2.187	0.015	0.05	0.073	0.127	0.531
CEQ	34,513	4,116	0.021	12.295	329.937	39.253	145.495	25,674.058
TQ	34,513	4,116	0.238	0.991	1.865	1.32	1.997	37.81

Note: Data on market capitalization, capital employed and equity book value are in the millions of dollars.

Chapter 3

Preliminary Data Analysis*

Abstract

This chapter first analyzes how the data-cleaning process affects the share of missing values in the extracted European and North American data-sets. It then moves on to examine how three different approaches to treat the issue of missing values, Complete Case, Multiple Imputation Chained Equations (MICE), and K-Nearest Neighbor (KNN) imputations affect the number of firms and their average lifespan in the datasets compared to the original sample and assessed across different SIC industry divisions. This is extended to consider implied effects on the distribution of a key performance indicator, return on assets (ROA), calculating skewness and kurtosis measures for each of the treatment methods and across industry contexts. This consistently shows highly negatively skewed distributions with high positive excess kurtosis across all the industries where the KNN imputation treatment creates results with distribution characteristics that are closest to the original untreated data. We further analyze the persistency of the (extreme) left-skewed tails measured in terms of the share of outliers and extreme outliers, which shows consistent and rather high percentages of outliers around 15% of the full sample and extreme outliers around 7.5% indicating pervasive skewness in the data. Of the three alternative approaches to deal with missing values, the KNN imputation treatment is found to be the method that generates final datasets that most closely resemble the original data even though the Complete Case approach remains the norm in mainstream studies. One consequence of this is that most empirical studies are likely to underestimate the prevalence of extreme negative performance outcomes.

Keywords: Average lifespan; extreme outliers; kurtosis; negative tails; outliers; skewness

---

*Martin Albæk was instrumental in the ensuing analysis of the collected and treated datasets.

A Study of Risky Business Outcomes: Adapting to Strategic Disruption, 29–45
Copyright © 2023 by Torben Juul Andersen
Published under exclusive licence by Emerald Publishing Limited
doi:10.1108/978-1-83797-074-220231003

Introduction

The previous chapter presented the theoretical and technical foundations for alternative approaches to deal with missing values adopted in our treatment of the collected datasets. We used this to assess the effects of three different approaches adopting the Complete Case, MICE, and KNN mean techniques. In this chapter we compare the datasets and the distributions of key variables derived from these three different ways of dealing with missing values in view of the characteristics of the original information obtained from the datasets. The following simplifies an otherwise extensive analysis by confining the comparative analytics to the distribution characteristics of one key performance measure, ROA, which is one of the most commonly used performance indicators in empirical management studies. The comparative analysis looks across the complete case dataset and the two imputed datasets for each of the two geographical regions. The analyses are further refined by comparing the data characteristics across different industry contexts.

Analyzing Missing Values

To limit what might otherwise become an extensive analysis, we focus on a single key performance variable subjected to comparative analyses between the two datasets as refined and treated by three different approaches adopted to deal with the missing data issue. We chose to analyze ROA, not because it necessarily is the best-performance indicator but because it is one of the most widely used return measures in mainstream management research and therefore of key interest. The number of missing data values differs substantially between the European and the North American datasets. This difference is partially explained by the qualitative detail of the underlying data collection process and the various data-cleaning approaches adopted to deal with the missing values. As part of the data-cleaning process, firms that had more than 50% of missing values in at least one of the reporting years were dropped as these companies were considered inadmissible for proper execution of the imputation techniques. A value was conceived as missing, if it "truly" was absent, was considered too extreme, or "impossible" but yet deemed viable for recreation, or replacement with an alternative value deemed tenable for imputation. The amount of extreme and missing values on ROA in the North American dataset are mostly concentrated on companies that have been entirely dropped from the sample, thus leaving a relatively small percentage (0.3%) in the final dataset. In the European dataset this is not quite the case, so a substantial share of the missing values (13.4%) remains in the final dataset. However, we see substantial differences in the share of missing values between the two geographical regions across the various performance variables reflecting differences in recording quality in the two datasets (Table 3.1).

From this vantage point, we proceed to analyze the differences observed in the distribution of ROA across the three different treatment approaches, Complete Case, MICE, and KNN imputations in the datasets for each of the two geographical regions, Europe and North America. We first look at the number

Table 3.1.   Shares of Missing Values for Each Performance Variable by Geographical Area.

Variable	Missing Values Per Variable (%)	
	Europe (%)	North America (%)
Return on assets	13.4	0.3
Market capitalization	3.6	9.8
Operating margin	16.0	6.8
Capital employed	1.1	13.4
Cash flow returns	5.4	3.1
Equity book value	2.8	5.9
Tobin's Q	6.0	9.9

Note: The table is construed by analyzing missing values in the full dataset (after dropping firms with more than 50% of missing values) looking at each of the performance variables separately, *roa, mktcap, opm, ce, cfre, ceq, tq.*

of (public) firms across different industries and their average lifespan (years) of the company as recorded in Compustat before assessing effects on distribution skewness and kurtosis derived from each of the treatment approaches chosen to deal with missing values while also examining observed effects on the number of outliers in the datasets.

Analyzing Number of Firms and Their Lifespans

Firms may stop reporting data and be part of the datasets if they go bankrupt, but there can be (many) other reasons, such as that the company is delisted to go private, or is being acquired by another firm and therefore delisted. Our analyses therefore only focuses on the behavior of firms while they are formally registered as public listed company, and we do not have explicit information on the fate of companies that are no longer included in the dataset.

The number of firms comprised in the datasets and their average lifespans as public registered companies varies for each geographical region and according to the approach adopted to deal with the missing values issue (Table 3.2, Panels A and B). The number of firms count how many companies are included in the dataset at some point over the 25-year period 1996–2019. The average public lifespan is calculated as the mean value of number of years a given firm has been recorded in the Compustat database and hence included in the dataset.

We observe that the number of firms decreases significantly across all industries from the original to the treated dataset when using the complete case approach (Table 3.2) and independently of geographical location, that is, it is seen in both the European (Panel A) and North American (Panel B) datasets. We further note that the MICE approach has the second highest number of firms deleted while the KNN approach retains the highest number of firms in the final dataset. We

Table 3.2. Number of Firms and Their Lifespan Across Different Treatments and Regions.

Panel A. European Dataset

	Europe							
	Number of Firms				Lifespan (Years)			
Sic Division	Original	Complete	MICE	KNN	Original	Complete	MICE	KNN
Agriculture, Forestry, Fishing	72	33	68	72	10.0	7.8	10.0	10.0
Finance, Insurance, and Real-estate	83	36	77	82	6.5	7.2	6.5	6.5
Manufacturing, Materials, Machines, etc.	2,358	1,009	2,315	2,321	10.8	8.9	10.8	10.8
Manufacturing, Food, Apparel, etc.	1,749	688	1,711	1,720	10.8	8.8	10.7	10.8
Mining and Construction	731	259	714	722	10.1	8.8	10.0	10.0
Other	2,393	1,240	2,323	2,332	9.3	7.8	9.2	9.2
Transportation, Communication, Distribution	958	409	942	940	10.2	8.2	10.1	10.2
Wholesale and Retail	944	442	926	933	10.1	8.6	10.1	10.1

Table 3.2. (*Continued*)

Panel B. North American Dataset

	North America							
	Number of Firms				Lifespan (Years)			
Sic Division	Original	Complete	MICE	KNN	Original	Complete	MICE	KNN
Agriculture, Forestry, Fishing	61	26	60	61	10.3	10.2	10.3	10.3
Finance, Insurance, and Real-estate	2,225	148	1,913	2,225	10.3	8.6	9.9	10.3
Manufacturing, Materials, Machines, etc.	3,324	1,476	3,033	3,324	11.5	12.0	11.4	11.5
Manufacturing, Food, Apparel, etc.	2,314	766	2,049	2,314	10.7	11.8	10.7	10.7
Mining and Construction	1,714	503	1,602	1,714	9.9	9.4	9.6	9.9
Other	2,921	802	2,555	2,921	9.2	8.8	9.0	9.2
Transportation, Communication, Distribution	1,593	506	1,504	1,593	11.8	11.5	11.8	11.8
Wholesale and Retail	1,367	571	1,260	1,367	10.6	10.3	10.6	10.6

also see that industries in the agriculture, forestry, and fishing sectors have the lowest number of public firms, whereas industry sectors in manufacturing, materials, and machines hold the highest number of public companies in the imputed North American and European datasets.

Looking at the lifespan of firm (average number of years registered), we see that it tends to only barely change when applying the MICE and KNN approaches as only relatively few companies are dropped in these processes. Conversely, the lifespan of firms decreases dramatically when the complete case approach is followed. In fact, for the European dataset, across all industry sectors, except agriculture, forestry and fishing, the average lifespan appears to drop by almost two years (Table 3.2). In the case of the North American dataset (Panel B), the impact of the complete case approach is mixed, as the lifespan decreases in some industries whereas it increases in other industries. This means that in the European dataset (Panel A) the complete case approach causes the largest and longest registered firms to be dropped from the final dataset, leaving those with less years of registration in the sample. This will make analytical derivations and conclusions from regression analysis based on the complete case sample less reliable for longer-lasting companies. It may therefore compromise the representativeness of the dataset and also hamper efforts to study the behaviors of outlying firms that outperform and underperform. It seems fairly safe to assume that consistently outperforming firms also correspond to those companies that tend to survive for the longest periods of time, so by cutting off those companies from the sample we are probably also eliminating interesting over-performing organizations.

In general, the average lifespan of companies in the European dataset converges around 10 years across all the industries and across all three adopted treatments to deal with missing values, except for the finance, insurance, and real-estate industry with an average lifespan of around seven years, and the complete case approach that posts average lifespans of around eight years. In the North American dataset, on the other hand, the average lifespan seems to be more consistent across industries hovering around 10.5 years within a range of 8.6 and 11.8 and compared to the European dataset, it appears to retain the larger and longer-lasting firms.

Analyzing Distribution Characteristics

We analyze the skewness and kurtosis of the performance distributions measured by ROA in each of the two datasets for Europe and North America. Skewness and kurtosis are statistical measures that capture two different distribution characteristics. The skewness measure relates to the third moment of the distribution taking a value of zero when the distribution is normally distributed, where negative outcomes have the same probability of happening as the positive outcomes (e.g., Hair, Black, Babin, & Anderson, 2010; Hull, 2018; Wooldridge, 2010). If the skewness is positive, it implies that very high returns are more likely and very low returns are less likely compared to a normal distribution. Conversely, when the skewness is negative the opposite is true, and implies that very low returns are much more likely and very high returns less likely. The kurtosis measure relates to the fourth moment of the distribution and takes on the value of 3, if the distribution is normally distributed. Hence, when authors in the finance literature talk about excess kurtosis they refer to distributions that to some degree fail to fulfill the expected contours of a normal distribution, that is, it indicates the degree to which the kurtosis of a given distribution deviates from and exceeds 3 as the norm for the normally distributed ideal.

If excess kurtosis is positive and well above 3, it means that both very high and very low returns are more likely to occur compared to predictions from a normal distribution. If excess kurtosis is negative, that is, well below 3, it means that very high and very low returns are less likely compared to a normal distribution thereby displaying a narrower range of possible outcomes. The skewness and kurtosis of an invested portfolio influences the expected return. That is, if an investor is pricing a portfolio believing its returns are normally distributed when in fact they are negatively skewed with positive excess kurtosis, it means the investor is underestimating the likelihood of realizing extreme negative returns from the investment. By implication, the investor will price the portfolio at a higher value than would be the case if the "true" distribution was known.

The analysis shows that skewness always is negative, across geographical regions, industry sectors, and for all treatments of missing values (Table 3.3) except in two instances in the Agriculture, Forestry, and Fishing sectors in Europe and the Finance, Insurance, and Real-estate sectors in North America when applying the MICE approach. This illustrates one of the limitations of the MICE imputation methodology, namely that the skewness can change (at times dramatically) compared to the original dataset. The same argument can also be applied to the Complete Case approach as this method seems to reduce the skewness significantly across all the industries except the Mining and Construction sectors.

By comparison, the KNN approach retains the skewness almost unchanged across the board compared to the original dataset (Table 3.3). If we look at the kurtosis, we note that it always exceeds the value 3 as the threshold of a normal distribution, and in some instances is dramatically above the threshold value. This means that there generally is high positive excess kurtosis in the performance data indicating the presence of extreme returns in the distribution way beyond the limits suggested by the commonly assumed normal distribution. Also in this case, the datasets derived from the MICE imputation and the Complete Case approaches provide the values that are furthest away from the original dataset whereas the KNN approach leaves the kurtosis almost at the same level as the original dataset.

These results seem to imply that the Complete Case approach tends to drop companies with extreme and negative values, since its skewness is more positive and the kurtosis lower compared to the original dataset. The MICE imputation approach tends to substitute the missing values with more extreme values, which increases the kurtosis of the final dataset, where the incoherent changes in skewness across various industries seem to suggest that the imputed values take on both extremely positive and negative values as the case may be.

Table 3.3.   Skewness and Kurtosis of ROA Distribution across Treatments and Regions.

Panel A. Skewness and Kurtosis in the European Dataset

| | Europe | | | | | | | |
| | Skewness | | | | Kurtosis | | | |
Sic Division	Original	Complete	MICE	KNN	Original	Complete	MICE	KNN
Agriculture, Forestry, Fishing	-5.3	-3.3	3.6	-5.7	38.7	15.0	124.3	43.9
Finance, Insurance, and Real-estate	-4.5	-1.9	-4.5	-5.0	28.1	7.3	30.0	35.1
Manufacturing, Materials, Machines, etc.	-5.3	-4.6	-21.9	-5.7	47.4	39.1	803.6	54.7
Manufacturing, Food, Apparel, etc.	-4.7	-3.5	-31.6	-5.1	35.3	20.2	1,838.3	41.9
Mining and Construction	-5.2	-9.1	-16.6	-5.4	39.3	129.2	523.3	42.2
Other	-5.2	-5.2	-39.6	-5.2	39.6	44.5	2,258.1	40.4
Transportation, Communication, Distribution	-7.8	-8.8	-92.2	-8.5	94.9	149.8	8,794.9	112.1
Wholesale and Retail	-5.7	-4.3	-76.6	-6.0	59.5	36.7	6,727.3	67.5

Table 3.3. (*Continued*)

Panel B. Skewness and Kurtosis in the North American Dataset

Sic Division	North America							
	Skewness				Kurtosis			
	Original	Complete	MICE	KNN	Original	Complete	MICE	KNN
Agriculture, Forestry, Fishing	−13.0	−4.7	−2.6	−13.0	186.7	41.1	24.5	187.3
Finance, Insurance, and Real-estate	−29.2	−11.2	35.2	−29.1	1,551.4	224.1	4,096.9	1,547.0
Manufacturing, Materials, Machines, etc.	−18.3	−7.4	−17.8	−18.3	632.4	125.5	554.4	631.3
Manufacturing, Food, Apparel, etc.	−16.7	−6.3	−21.7	−16.7	486.7	75.6	1,137.7	487.6
Mining and Construction	−18.6	−30.5	−17.8	−18.6	587.7	1,462.4	609.3	590.2
Other	−19.5	−8.9	−28.3	−19.5	603.6	168.5	2,469.5	603.1
Transportation, Communication, Distribution	−54.5	−21.0	−83.3	−54.5	4,471.0	832.1	9,203.9	4,480.8
Wholesale and Retail	−21.2	−6.2	−3.2	−21.1	623.5	80.4	1,110.5	619.3

The information also suggests that one should be cautious when using the Complete Case approach, as this final dataset implies a skewness that is consistently less negative, and a kurtosis that is lower than those values observed in the original datasets (Table 3.3). This implies that conclusions drawn from the dataset treated according to the Complete Case approach may assume that in extreme negative events, outcomes take place less frequently than what seems to in fact happen in reality. This may pose a problem for investment analysis, as explained above, but also challenges the validity of findings from statistical analyses that (typically can) underestimate the frequency of extreme (negative) outcomes. Finally, it is noted that the North American dataset seems to have more extreme, and negative exemplars among the registered firms compared to the European dataset over the time period of collected data, 1995–2019.

Analyzing Data Outliers

The last dimensions of the return distributions that we will investigate are those related to the occurrence of outlying values represented by firms referred to as the so-called outliers. An outlier is a firm that presents a value that differs substantially in size from the rest of the data observed in the collected sample. The outliers, or the extreme values they represent can be caused by disastrous organizational acts or by human reporting errors, where both instances can create unrealistic extreme values, particularly if these companies appear to be consistently under- or over-performing. Taking a closer look at the outliers is interesting and relevant as one purpose of this research project is to study performance outliers among representative firms.

The central question regarding how we define an "outlier" in turn requires that we determine what a "substantial" discrepancy means when we assess the data. Hence, we can decide to follow Tukey's (1977) approach to define the term outlier. He considers a data point to be an outlier if its value falls outside the range determined by $[1Q - 1.5\text{IQR}; 3Q + 1.5\text{IQR}]$, that is, the observation falls below the value $[1Q - 1.5\text{IQR}]$, where $1Q$ is the first quartile, or above the value $3Q + 1.5\text{IQR}]$, where $3Q$ is the third quartile, and IQR is the interquartile range $[\text{IQR} = 3Q - 1Q]]$ (Tukey, 1977). Hence, we apply a factor of 1.5 to substantiate and quantitatively determine an "outlier." To determine an "extreme outlier," we instead use a slightly higher coefficient of 3 instead of 1.5 in the Tukey (1977) outlier formula.

This method of identifying outliers is relatively simple and straightforward and it does not adopt dispersion measures like standard deviation to imply extreme potential outliers. Instead, the method defines "inner" and "outer" fences defined by quartiles that are not influenced by a few extreme observed values. While it is possible to devise a method to determine probabilities associated with the fences based on the cumulative distribution (Schwertman, Owens, & Adnan, 2004), we do not make any attempts to apply that in this analysis.

Based on the Tukey (1977) outlier definition, we calculate the frequencies of observed "outliers" and "extreme outliers" in the datasets for each of the two geographical regions and across all the different industry sectors by the treatment approach adopted to deal with missing values expressed as a percentage of outliers compared to the full dataset (Table 3.4). It can be seen that the Complete Case approach in most instances lead to a decrease in the share of outliers and extreme outliers across all industries. We further note that the KNN imputation approach reaches at a share of outliers and extreme outliers that is quite similar to the original dataset particularly in the North American dataset whereas the outcomes from the MICE imputation approach varies somewhat. In general, the share of outliers on average falls around 15% of all the observed data across industry sectors and treatment approaches dealing with missing values, whereas the extreme outliers hover around a 7.5% share of the original dataset.

More Fine-grained Analyses

As we expand the analyses further in a more fine-grained examination of the datasets updated with imputed values adopting the KNN and MICE techniques, we see some noticeable differences in performance measures between the geographical regions (North America and Europe) and across the imputation treatment approaches (see Appendix 3.1). ROA on the North American data show more variation with larger distance between minimum and maximum returns (−73.4%/46.6%) after the MICE treatment (Panel B) compared to (−68.8/24.8%) after the KNN treatment (Panel A). These results are repeated in the European dataset that also shows larger distance between minimum and maximum returns (−133.9%/7.1%) after the MICE treatment (Panel D) compared to (−22.7%/11.8%) after the KNN treatment (Panel C). That is, the MICE treatment leads to wider distributions with a higher potential for outliers in both geographical regions although the North American dataset has a wider range of outcomes in comparison to the European dataset, at least after the KNN treatment, whereas the MICE treatment appears to make the European dataset somewhat more erratic.

Looking across the comparable return measures, such as, operating margin (OPM) and cash flow returns (CFRE), the North American data show huge distances between minimum and maximum OPM (−275.3%/160.6%) after the MICE treatment (Panel B) compared to (834%/732,747%) after KNN treatment (Panel A). The European dataset also shows huge distances between minimum and maximum OPM values (−886%/690,011%) after the MICE treatment (Panel D) compared to (−1,685%/6,302%) after the KNN treatment (Panel C). These measures are clearly not satisfactory as these data treatment methods lead to extreme and unexpected deviations that are hard to explain and justify. The corresponding outcomes for cash flow returns in the North American data show wide distances between minimum and maximum CFRE (−79.1%/35.2%) after the MICE treatment (Panel B) compared to (−168.7%/48.8%) after the KNN treatment (Panel A). The European data also show distances between minimum and maximum CFRE of (−27.8%/2.0%) after the MICE treatment (Panel D) and (−2.2%/38.3%) after the KNN treatment (Panel C). The effects from the KNN and MICE treatments are not as extreme on CFRE compared to OPM and outcomes are more compatible with the outcomes found on ROA. On this basis we tentatively conclude that applying imputed data on operating margin (OPM) as

Table 3.4.   Outliers and Extreme Outliers of ROA across Treatments and Regions.

Panel A. Outliers and Extreme Outliers in the European Dataset

| | Europe | | | | | | | |
| | Outliers | | | | Extreme Outliers | | | |
Sic Division	Original (%)	Complete (%)	MICE (%)	KNN (%)	Original (%)	Complete (%)	MICE (%)	KNN (%)
Agriculture, Forestry, Fishing	14	9	13	15	7	4	6	8
Finance, Insurance, and Real-estate	22	18	21	16	12	9	12	10
Manufacturing, Materials, Machines, etc.	13	12	14	14	7	6	7	7
Manufacturing, Food, Apparel, etc.	14	12	15	16	8	6	8	9
Mining and Construction	10	10	11	11	5	4	6	5
Other	14	14	15	14	7	7	8	7
Transportation, Communication, Distribution	14	12	14	14	7	5	8	7
Wholesale and Retail	12	8	12	13	6	3	6	6

Table 3.4. (*Continued*)

Panel B. Outliers and extreme outliers in the North American Dataset

Sic Division	North America							
	Outliers				Extreme Outliers			
	Original (%)	Complete (%)	MICE (%)	KNN (%)	Original (%)	Complete (%)	MICE (%)	KNN (%)
Agriculture, Forestry, Fishing	14.5	9.1	13.5	14.6	6.7	3.4	5.3	6.7
Finance, Insurance, and Real-estate	18.5	12.7	16.8	18.7	11.4	6.0	10.0	11.6
Manufacturing, Materials, Machines, etc.	13.2	11.4	12.6	13.2	7.5	5.1	6.8	7.5
Manufacturing, Food, Apparel, etc.	9.9	13.2	11.7	9.9	4.5	6.5	5.2	4.5
Mining and Construction	10.9	9.1	10.9	10.9	5.9	3.9	5.8	5.9
Other	13.5	12.9	13.7	13.5	7.6	6.9	7.4	7.6
Transportation, Communication, Distribution	17.9	14.7	16.9	17.9	9.9	6.1	8.7	9.8
Wholesale and Retail	13.0	10.4	12.8	13.0	6.7	4.1	6.4	6.7

"Outliers" are defined here as those values that are either, lower than the difference between the first quartile and 1.5x IQR, where IQR is the interquartile range determined as the difference between the first and third quartile, or higher than the sum of the third quartile and 1.5x IQR.

"Extreme outliers" are defined following the same logic as applied to the definition of "outliers" except that IQR is multiplied by a factor of 3 instead of a factor of 1.5.

return measure is untenable, whereas the treated values for ROA and CFRE provide more consistent datasets.

Findings and Conclusion

The preceding data analyses portray persistent negative skewness in the distribution of financial return (ROA) and most of the time display a (sizeable) excess kurtosis showing a significant share of outliers corresponding to around 15% of the total dataset and extreme outliers constituting around 7.5% of the dataset. This is the case regardless of the choice of geographical region (North America and Europe), industry sectors (SIC), or the adopted treatment method to account for missing data (Complete, MICE, and KNN). This presents rather substantive deviations from an (often assumed) normal distribution of firm performance outcomes and thereby justifies our mounting curiosity about what might explain this seemingly persistent empirical artifact of very negatively skewed return distributions with substantial excess positive kurtosis that signify a high potential for extreme (negative) outliers. The analysis of the data peaks the curious question about (some of) the causes that can elucidate these performance disparities, and why this apparent consistency of extreme negatively skewed performance distributions prevail across industry contexts and geographical regions for such an extended period of time.

However, the underlying technical issues related to the treatment of missing values in the complete original data assembled from the Compustat sources remain unresolved and while we cannot expect a final verdict on this, a few notes are warranted. Looking at the distribution of the final datasets derived from the different treatment approaches adopted to deal with the missing data, it seems that the methodology displaying the most similar distribution characteristics to the original dataset, is the KNN imputation technique (Table 3.3, Panels A and B). The datasets that result from this methodology have characteristics that are quite close to the original data compared to any of the alternative Complete Case and the MICE imputation approaches. The KNN dataset has almost the same skewness, kurtosis, and shares of outliers and extreme outliers as the complete original datasets in both of the geographical regions. This places the KNN imputation treatment as a more ideal way of contending with the issue of missing values in empirical studies. We observe here with some caution how the MICE approach reaches at more extreme outcomes compared to the KNN approach particularly when considering an alternative return measure like operating margin (OPM). Hence, the KNN treatment seems to reproduce characteristics that more closely resemble those embedded in the true original data that the other approaches fail to reproduce.

With respect to the two other approaches of dealing with missing values, we note that the MICE treatment retains more firms in the final sample than does the Complete Case approach, but also makes (substantial) changes to the distribution characteristics of the datasets measured by skewness and kurtosis, which suggests that it imputes very extreme values for at least some of the missing values. Therefore, when choosing between the Complete Case and the MICE approaches, one must decide what to prioritize, whether it serves the analysis better to generate a larger sample size with (some) unrealistic (extreme) values, or a smaller data-set without any such naturally occurring values. However, the Complete Case approach eliminates many of the extreme observations registered in the original dataset and may therefore underestimate the role of extreme events and outcomes in empirical studies. Nevertheless, the Complete Case approach remains predominant in many empirical studies published in the management field.

A final, and not insignificant, insight gained from this analysis of the performance data derived from the extensive Compustat datasets is that what is consistently observed in the North American data with respect to extreme negatively skewed financial returns is replicated in the European data. While a majority of empirical studies historically have been based on North American data, partly out of convenience and partly out of tradition, we observe the same general phenomena in an extensive data sample of European firms. This may suggest an increased focus on future studies that use European data to complement what has already been published based on North American data.

In the ensuing chapter, we will extend this preliminary data analysis and enter into more extended investigations of the observed performance phenomena.

References

Hair, J., Black, W. C., Babin, B. J., & Anderson, R. E. (2010). *Multivariate data analysis* (7th ed.). Upper Saddle River, NJ: Pearson Education International.

Hull, J. C. (2018). *Risk management and financial institutions* (5th ed.). Hoboken, NJ: Wiley.

Tukey, J. W. (1977). *Exploratory data analysis.* Boston, MA: Addison-Wesley.

Schwertman, N. C., Owens, M. A., & Adnan, R. (2004). A simple more general boxplot method for identifying outliers. *Computational Statistics & Data Analysis*, *47*(1), 165–174.

Wooldridge, J. M. (2010). *Econometric analysis of cross section and panel data* (2nd ed.). Cambridge, MA: MIT Press.

Appendix 3.1.   The Effect of Imputation Treatments on Each Geographical Dataset

Panel A: North America KNN Treatment

	Obs. (1)	Companies (2)	Min. (3)	1st Qu. (4)	Mean (5)	Median (6)	3rd Qu. (7)	Max. (8)
mktCAP	156,576	14,960	0.0009	28.696	2,453.148	165.6	945.133	1,551,633.6
ROA	156,576	14,960	−68.802	−0.048	−0.058	0.021	0.063	24.84
OPM	156,576	14,960	−275.286	0.014	−0.818	0.11	0.226	160.612
CE	156,576	14,960	0.032	29.319	2,660.243	164.106	1,018.366	1,214,093.9
CFRE	156,576	14,960	−168.713	−0.004	0.022	0.059	0.115	48.827
CEQ	156,576	14,960	0.025	20.631	946.912	95.84	488.828	48,121.89
TQ	156,576	14,960	0.0007	0.989	2.758	1.315	2.08	5,099.97

Panel B: North America MICE Treatment

	Obs. (1)	Companies (2)	Min. (3)	1st Qu. (4)	Mean (5)	Median (6)	3rd Qu. (7)	Max. (8)
mktCAP	145,631	13,976	0.0009	36.642	2,607.56	203.792	1,139.428	1,547,896
ROA	145,631	13,976	−73.444	−0.037	−0.056	0.024	0.065	46.577
OPM	145,631	13,976	−4,823,443	0.03	−485.327	0.119	0.241	732,747.19
CE	145,631	13,976	0.02	33.835	3,813.336	196.554	1,136.776	1,442,251.4
CFRE	145,631	13,976	−79.113	0.002	0.024	0.063	0.118	35.172
CEQ	145,631	13,976	0.009	23.979	1,188.777	112.831	550.678	1,108,387
TQ	145,631	13,976	0.004	1.022	2.729	1.353	2.088	8,831.687

Appendix 3.1. *(Continued)*

Panel C: Europe KNN Treatment

	Obs. (1)	Companies (2)	Min. (3)	1st Qu. (4)	Mean (5)	Median (6)	3rd Qu. (7)	Max. (8)
mktCAP	92,913	9,154	0.0006	17.079	1,870.89	72.855	380.753	2,159,842.4
ROA	92,913	9,154	−22.73	−0.014	−0.011	0.03	0.065	11.791
OPM	92,913	9,154	−1,685	0.031	−0.374	0.091	0.164	6,302.47
CE	92,913	9,154	0.087	18.314	999.035	69.711	338.937	65,993.5
CFRE	92,913	9,154	−2.2	0.008	0.049	0.068	0.119	38.269
CEQ	92,913	9,154	0.019	13.706	523.888	48.683	207.869	29,943.48
TQ	92,913	9,154	0.0008	0.93	2.183	1.233	1.873	4,707.185

Panel D: Europe MICE Treatment

	Obs. (1)	Companies (2)	Min. (3)	1st Qu. (4)	Mean (5)	Median (6)	3rd Qu. (7)	Max. (8)
mktCAP	91,909	9,076	0.003	17.553	1,639.9	73.065	375.365	1,794,847
ROA	91,909	9,076	−133.89	−0.023	−0.038	0.029	0.066	7.096
OPM	91,909	9,076	−8,394,898	−0.036	−162.49	0.033	0.096	690,011
CE	91,909	9,076	0.085	18.053	1,012.5	71.119	349.881	85,467
CFRE	91,909	9,076	−27.837	0.005	0.032	0.065	0.117	2.001
CEQ	91,909	9,076	0.019	13.695	547.06	50.147	214.616	73,637
TQ	91,909	9,076	0.001	0.949	2.246	1.236	1.843	1,950.1

Chapter 4

Extended Data Analysis[*]

Abstract

This chapter takes a closer look at outliers and extreme outliers identified
in the data derived from a complete case treatment of missing values in
the European and North American datasets and consistently observe significant negatively skewed distributions with high excess kurtosis across all
industries. We then plot the density functions for return on assets (ROA)
across different industries in the two datasets and find pervasive observations in the tails where negative returns and outlying observations constitute a frequent and recurring phenomenon. We analyze the persistency of
outliers and find noticeable percentages of outlying over- and underperformers hovering around 3–6% dependent on industry context. We further
analyze potential size effects associated with extreme negative skewness but
do not find that (even sizeable) elimination of extreme values reduce the
phenomenon. Finally, we analyze the percentage of firm observations that
must be eliminated to reach at distributions that fulfill the characteristics
of a normal distribution and reach at a substantial percentage of around
5–10% dependent on industry. To conclude, the often-assumed normally
distributed performance outcomes are typically wrong and discards the
substantial number of outliers in the samples.

Keywords: Consistent negative tails; extreme values; persistent outliers;
pervasive excess kurtosis; size effects; winsorization

Introduction

The previous chapters introduced three different ways of dealing with the
problem of missing values in the collected datasets, and we observed how

---

[*]Martin Albæk was instrumental in conducting the ensuing analyses of the collected
and treated datasets.

A Study of Risky Business Outcomes: Adapting to Strategic Disruption, 47–65
Copyright © 2023 by Torben Juul Andersen
Published under exclusive licence by Emerald Publishing Limited
doi:10.1108/978-1-83797-074-220231004

the different approaches of complete case and various imputation techniques affect the final datasets and observed outliers. From this we concluded that the complete case approach significantly reduces the number of observations and retained outliers in the final datasets. Despite this shortcoming, the complete case approach remains the norm in mainstream finance and management studies, so we adopt this approach in the extended analysis of outliers performed in this chapter.

The study of outliers and the nature of the firms they represent remain a key focus in this research project and by adopting a complete case approach, we can therefore argue that we assume a rather "conservative" stance in the identification of outliers for our study. There are several definitions of the outlier concept and we apply Tukey's (1977) quartile approach discussed in the previous chapter (see Chapter 3). This captures performance measures that fall in the (extreme) tails of the return distributions and thus identifies firms that appear to represent excessively low- or high-performance outcomes compared to the general population (e.g., Schwertman, Owens, & Adnan, 2004). The statistical measure kurtosis tells us something about the relative likelihood, or frequency of observing extreme outcomes in the distribution tails. The higher the excessive positive kurtosis is (above the value 3), the more leptokurtic is the distribution and the more likely it is to find observations in the extreme tails. The statistical skewness measure tells us some things about whether, and to what extent we can expect outliers in either of the negative or the positive tails of the distribution. A positive skewness measure (above +1 and higher) increases the likelihood of finding extreme outliers in the positive tail of the performance distribution whereas a negative skewness measure (below −1 and lower) increases the likelihood of finding extreme outliers in the negative tail of the distribution.

Analyzing Outliers and Distributions

Here we examine the performance outliers determined by the distribution characteristics of ROA, or financial returns observed across industry sectors in each of the two regional datasets for Europe and North America, respectively. The ensuing analyses examine the frequency diagrams for this commonly applied performance variable and assesses the existence (and persistency) of identified outliers in the two geographical samples noting possible size effects and considering how far the samples are from displaying the contours of a normal distribution. We do this by counting how many extreme observations must be dropped to bring the remaining data into fulfillment of the general normality assumptions.

Using the complete case dataset is considered the most reasonable starting point for this analysis given the prominence (still) afforded to this approach in the extant empirical literature. Hence, we do this in recognition of its prominence as a most commonly adopted and generally accepted approach to deal with missing values in the social sciences even though this approach also drops the highest number of outliers among the alternative techniques discussed and examined in the prior chapters (see Chapters 2 and 3).

We compare the complete case sample to the original dataset as a natural basis of reference to assess the effects of this particular way of treating the missing values. The complete case dataset is based on deflated values where all annual figures use 1995 as a comparable reference, which makes the data easy to compare across each year over the 25-year sample period 1995–2019.

We observe how the complete case approach decreases the number of outliers, extreme outliers, skewness, and kurtosis somewhat across all industries, both in the European and the North American datasets (Table 4.1). On average the share of outliers across industries in the European dataset drop from 14.1% of the original sample to 11.9% whereas the average share of extreme outliers is reduced from 7.4% to 5.5%.[1]

These changes in numbers correspond to decreases in the share of outliers and extreme outliers of around 15% and 25%, respectively, when applying the complete case approach to deal with missing values. By comparison, the average share of outliers across industries in the North American dataset drops from 13.9% of the original sample to 11.7% and average share of extreme outliers from 7.5% to 5.3% corresponding to decreases in the share of outliers and extreme outliers of around 16% and 30%, respectively.

The average skewness measure taken across the noted industries in the European dataset drops from −5.5 in the original sample to −5.1 in the complete case dataset whereas the average kurtosis measure increases from 47.9 to 55.2 (Table 4.1). By comparison the average skewness measure across industries in the North American dataset drops from −23.9 in the original sample to −12.0 in the complete case dataset while average kurtosis falls from 1,142 to 376. We note that the average skewness and kurtosis measures are considerably higher in the North American dataset compared to the European dataset. Hence, the most substantive reductions in negative skewness and positive kurtosis from the complete case treatment occurs in the North American dataset although the measures remain very prominent and significant in both the regional datasets.

That is, even after having applied the complete case approach, the negative skewness and positive kurtosis measures retain their substantive proportions in the treated datasets. A possible explanation for the extreme kurtosis and skewness might be that the performance distribution is influenced by only a few extreme negative values whereas the remainder of the observed values follow a normal distribution. To assess this possibility, we develop visual plots that allow us to examine the frequency distribution of the financial return data.

Figs. 4.1 and 4.2 show the performance distributions indicated by ROA across different industries in the European and North American datasets. These plots were created on the basis of R programming with the aim to visually examine whether the skewness and kurtosis are affected by just a few isolated extreme (negative) values or appear to constitute more pervasive phenomena. The graphs show the distribution of ROA for each SIC Division in the European and North

---

[1]Please note that these constitute simple unweighted averages of the reported numbers in Table 4.1.

Table 4.1.   Comparing Original European and North American Data with the Complete Dataset.

Panel A. European Data

Sic Division	Outliers Original (%)	Outliers Complete (%)	Extreme Outliers Original (%)	Extreme Outliers Complete (%)	Europe Skewness Original	Europe Skewness Complete	Europe Kurtosis Original	Europe Kurtosis Complete
Agriculture, Forestry, Fishing	14	9	7	4	-5.3	-3.3	38.7	15.0
Finance, Insurance, and Real-estate	22	18	12	9	-4.5	-1.9	28.1	7.3
Manufacturing, Materials, Machines, etc.	13	12	7	6	-5.3	-4.6	47.4	39.1
Manufacturing, Food, Apparel, etc.	14	12	8	6	-4.7	-3.5	35.3	20.2
Mining and Construction	10	10	5	4	-5.2	-9.1	39.3	129.2
Transportation, Communication, Distribution	14	12	7	5	-7.8	-8.8	94.9	149.8
Wholesale and Retail	12	8	6	3	-5.7	-4.3	59.5	36.7
Other	14	14	7	7	-5.2	-5.2	39.6	44.5

Panel B. North American Data

	North America							
	Outliers		Extreme Outliers		Skewness		Kurtosis	
Sic Division	Original (%)	Complete (%)	Original (%)	Complete (%)	Original	Complete	Original	Complete
Agriculture, Forestry, Fishing	14.5	9.1	6.7	3.4	−13.0	−4.7	186.7	41.1
Finance, Insurance, and Real-estate	18.5	12.7	1,4	6.0	−29.2	−11.2	1,551.4	224.1
Manufacturing, Materials, Machines, etc.	13.2	11.4	7.5	5.1	−18.3	−7.4	632.4	125.5
Manufacturing, Food, Apparel, etc.	9.9	13.2	4.5	6.5	−16.7	−6.3	486.7	75.6
Mining and Construction	10.9	9.1	5.9	3.9	−18.6	−30.5	587.7	1,462.4
Transportation, Communication, Distribution	17.9	14.7	9.9	6.1	−54.5	−21.0	4,471.0	832.1
Wholesale and Retail	13.0	10.4	6.7	4.1	−21.2	−6.2	623.5	80.4
Other	13.5	12.9	7.6	6.9	−19.5	−8.9	603.6	168.5

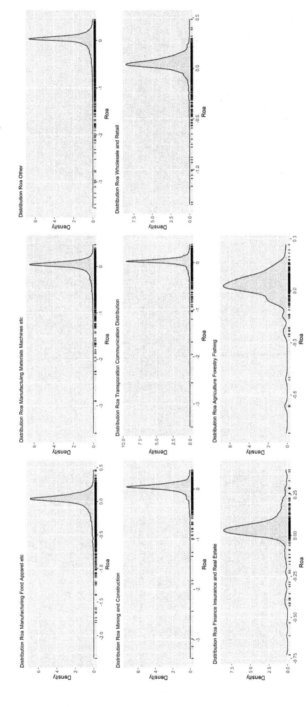

Fig. 4.1.   The ROA Distributions (Frequency Diagrams) in the European Dataset for Specific Industries (SIC Divisions). *Note:* Each of the vertical bar lines shown along the bottom (*x*-axis) of the frequency distribution diagrams represents one company (ROA) observation.

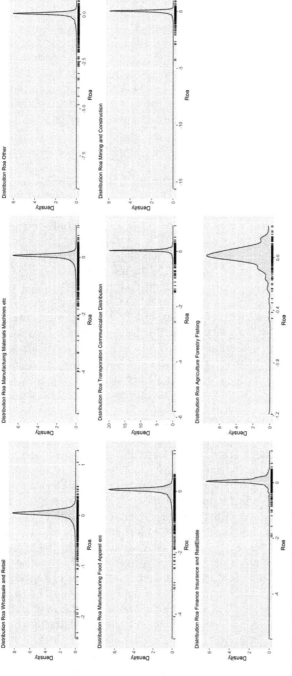

Fig. 4.2. The ROA Distributions (Frequency Diagrams) in the North American Dataset for Specific Industries (SIC Divisions). *Note*: Each of the vertical bar lines shown along the bottom (x-axis) of the frequency distribution diagrams represents one company (ROA) observation.

American datasets. Each vertical line plotted underneath at the bottom line (*x*-axis) in the distribution density graphic represents a single return observation from a company within the industry.

As it appears from the graphical displays, the most extreme values are concentrated in the negative end of the outcome scale. Moreover, these negative values do not seem to represent "isolated" observations in the sense that between the most extreme value and the value 0 there are really no big "gaps" but we observe a continuous presence of negative values although with some distance between observed values. This suggests that companies with negative returns constitute a frequent and recurring phenomenon that warrants further studies.

Analyzing Persistency of Outliers

A further examination of the data reveals that quite a sizeable proportion of the outliers are fairly persistent and constitute continuously underperforming, or over-performing firms. Table 4.2 illustrates the persistence of outlier firms in the complete case datasets for Europe and North America. The information on "absolute number of firms" registered in the table was created in the following way. For each five-year time bin over the 25-year sampling period, the top 5% and the lowest 5% performing companies measured by the distribution of their ROA measure are recorded for each SIC Division. Each time bin contains five years, starting with the first interval from 1995 until 1999, then 2000–2004, and so forth until 2015–2019. Hence, there are a total of five time bins in the full 25-year-long datasets.

For each SIC Division, we calculated how many times a company appeared only among the top performing firms ("Only Top"), how many times companies appeared both among the top performers and underperformers ("Both Bottom Top"), and finally how many times companies appeared only among the underperforming firms ("Only Bottom"). From this, we determined how many companies appeared more than once among the top 5% of performing firms ("Persistent Top"), and how many companies appeared more than once in the bottom 5% of performing firms ("Persistent Bottom"). The "Mean Companies Time Bin" column shows on average how many firms are included per time bin within a given SIC Division. Finally, the "Percentage of firms per industry per time bin" is calculated as the ratio between the relevant column from the "Absolute number of firms" and the "Mean Companies Time Bin" column to indicate the ratio of firms that fall within each of the headings, "Only Top," "Both Bottom Top," Only Bottom," "Persistent Top," and "Persistent Bottom."

As we observe from Table 4.2 (Panel A) around 4% of the companies have been top performers for at least two years in the European dataset, almost in all the industries. There is more variation when it comes to persistent bottom-performing companies, where the sectors of agriculture, forestry and fishing, and finance, insurance, and real estate have the lowest percentage of persistent bottom companies around 2%, while whole and retail, and manufacturing, materials, and machines have the highest share of bottom performers around 4.9% and 4.6%, respectively. In the North American dataset (Panel B) the situation is reversed. Here the percentage of companies being persistently among the bottom

Table 4.2. The Persistence of Outliers (Based on ROA) in the European and North American Complete Case Datasets.

Panel A: European Dataset Persistence of Outliers

SIC Division	Absolute Number of Firms					Mean Companies Per Time Bin	Percentage of Firms Per Industry Per Time Bin (%)				
	Only Top	Both Bottom Top	Only Bottom Top	Persistent Top	Persistent Bottom		Only Top	Both Bottom Top	Only Bottom Top	Persistent Top	Persistent Bottom
Agriculture, Forestry, Fishing	4	1	7	2	1	51	7.84	1.96	13.73	3.92	1.96
Finance, Insurance, and Real Estate	7	1	5	2	1	51	13.73	1.96	9.8	3.92	1.96
Manufacturing, Materials, Machines, etc.	137	34	166	74	81	1,780	7.7	1.91	9.33	4.16	4.55
Manufacturing, Food, Apparel, etc.	102	14	112	53	60	1,200	8.5	1.17	9.33	4.42	5
Mining and Construction	41	12	50	21	21	456	8.99	2.63	10.96	4.61	4.61
Transportation, Communication, Distribution	54	15	76	26	27	664	8.13	2.26	11.45	3.92	4.07
Wholesale and Retail	55	17	91	32	37	750	7.33	2.27	12.13	4.27	4.93
Other	170	31	213	88	104	1,920	8.85	1.61	11.09	4.58	5.42

(continued)

Panel B: North American Dataset Persistence of Outliers

SIC Division	Absolute Number of Firms						Percentage of Firms Per Industry Per Time Bin (%)				
	Only Top	Both Bottom Top	Only Bottom Top	Persistent Top	Persistent Bottom	Mean Companies Time Bin	Only Top	Both Bottom Top	Only Bottom Top	Persistent Top	Persistent Bottom
Agriculture, Forestry, Fishing	5	2	7	1	2	52	9.62	3.85	13.46	1.92	3.85
Finance, Insurance, and Real Estate	15	6	24	7	9	252	5.69	2.44	9.76	3.25	3.66
Manufacturing, Materials, Machines, etc.	254	134	250	122	122	3,491	7.36	3.85	7.21	3.48	3.51
Manufacturing, Food, Apparel, etc.	126	44	120	61	69	1,788	7.17	2.3	6.77	3.58	3.81
Mining and Construction	80	35	103	40	36	942	8.49	3.72	10.93	4.25	3.82
Transportation, Communication, Distribution	62	35	108	29	43	1,160	5.3	3.04	9.21	2.52	3.82
Wholesale and Retail	64	29	141	36	45	1,139	5.62	2.55	12.38	3.16	3.95
Other	110	54	122	42	54	1,382	7.94	3.9	8.74	3.03	3.97

The "Absolute number of firms" show how many firms belong to each industry classification.

The "Mean Companies Time Bin" column shows on average how many firms there are per time bin for a given SIC division, where each time bin contains five years, starting from 1995 until 2019 making up a total of five time bins.

The "Percentage of firms per industry per time bin" indicates the ratio between the "Absolute number of firms" and the "Mean Companies Time Bin" expressed as a percentage.

performers is fairly constant around 3.8% across all industries with the percentage of persistent top companies varies across industries, with mining and construction showing the highest percentage at 4.25%, and agriculture forestry and fishing the lowest at only around 1.9%.

It is frequently argued that persistently poor performance is associated with small "shaky" start-up companies whereas persistently superior performance is ascribed to large well-established industry leaders. Hence, it is pertinent to investigate whether there are such "size effects" at play in the presence of persistent outliers in the two datasets. Following this theoretical reasoning, smaller start-up companies will have higher variation in performance, so we would expect that if these smaller firms are dropped from the sample, there would be fewer extreme values observed and therefore a lower ratio of outliers. In the following we examine whether this logical reasoning pertains to the extensive data samples we have collected, or we need to look for deeper explanations than these "simple" and commonly promoted reasons.

We analyze this phenomenon, by looking at the extent to which the share of outliers and extreme outliers change, and if so how, depending on whether or not we include the smaller companies in the total samples. For instance, the datasets relative to the categories ">5 millions," ">15 millions," and ">30 millions" (Table 4.3) determined by the size of the firm's total assets, exclude observations for all the firms that have total assets below the indicated threshold values of 5, 15, and 30 million, respectively, with all values deflated to their 1995 levels.

As can be observed from Table 4.3, the percentage of outliers seem to barely change when the "smaller" firms with lower size of total assets are excluded from the two datasets from Europe (Panel A) and North America (Panel B). The percentage of "Outliers" and "Extreme Outliers" (almost) continue to hover between 8–14% and 4–6% of the samples, respectively, disregarding the exclusion of smaller firms, as observed across the various industries. More detailed analysis reveals that some (relatively small marginal) effects on the percentage of outliers arise when companies with less than 15 million in assets are dropped from the samples. For example, in the SIC Division "Finance Insurance and Real Estate" the percentage of outliers go from 18.1% to 12.8% when we impose this size criteria as the cutoff. However, if we apply this cutoff on both geographical datasets, we only loose an average 15% of total observations while the share of observations that are noted as outliers ("Out") and extreme outliers ("Extreme") remain above 10% and 4% of the total number of observations.

What is more, the percentage of outliers ("Out") also barely changes when the 30 million cutoff point is applied although with some differences noted across the different industry sectors. However, this cutoff point eliminates 25% of the total observations in the European dataset, whereas the North American dataset "only" is reduced by 20% of the total observations while still constituting some sizeable parts of the samples that yet are eliminated to little avail in terms of reducing the relative number performance outliers.

This analysis clearly demonstrates that the number of observations registered as performance outliers, and extreme outliers, is not explained by a size effect. That is, the outlier phenomenon around negatively skewed distributions of financial returns (ROA) are linked to issues that are independent from the size of the firm, which might exist, but (many) other things seems to be in play to explain this regularly observed phenomenon.

Analyzing Normality Criteria

To continue the analysis of the datasets, we thought it would be interesting to see how many extreme observations we needed to drop in order for the collected values on financial returns (ROA) to reach a distribution that lives up to the normality criteria in each of the SIC Divisions. The normality assumption is an important feature in a majority of social sciences papers that apply ordinary least square regression analysis and the like to determine whether statistically significant model relationships can be revealed from collected data. However, the use of these statistical techniques assumes that the performance distributions, or the residuals using them as dependent variables are approximately normally distributed.

A common approach applied to satisfy this requirement is to gradually eliminate the (extreme) outliers from the sample in a way that transforms the distribution of outcomes by limiting extreme values in the data and thereby reduce the effect of extraordinary, or unusual observations. As an example, this can be done by excluding performance variables with return values that fall beyond plus or minus three (or four) times the standard deviation around the mean, or by applying other standardized techniques to winsorize the data. It may also exclude all values outside a specific percentile of the data where, for example, a 90% winsorization of the data eliminates all values below the 5th percentile and above the 95th percentile. The process could also assign lower weights to the outlying observations and thereby change their values so they fall closer to the central data points in the sample.

Hence, we wanted to see how many, or how large a share of the outlying observations should be dropped from the sample to make the remaining observations reach levels of kurtosis and skewness in the distribution that falls within the limits of a normal distribution. To do this, we considered two alternative interpretations of what constitutes a "normal distribution" adopting two different definitions (a loose and a narrow definition) to assess the two geographical datasets. The first definition, the looser one, argues that the negative skewness measure must not fall below the value of −2 and the positive excess kurtosis must not exceed the value of 4. The other definition, the narrower and more conservative approach, argues that the negative skewness and excess kurtosis in the sample must not fall below a value of −0.5 and exceed a maximum value of 2, respectively. That is, we wanted to see how many, or how large a proportion of the outlying observations should be dropped from the samples to make the remaining data points reach levels of kurtosis and skewness that are commensurate with assumptions about normally distributed observations.

Table 4.4 (Panels A.1 and B.1) shows the needed percentage change in number of companies and observations to reach at satisfactory normality criteria according to the looser definition (skewness < 2; kurtosis < 4). In the case of the

Table 4.3. ROA Outliers in the North American and European Datasets Across Different Company Sizes.

Panel A: European Dataset (Share of Outliers and Extreme Outliers for Different Size Companies Determined by Total Assets)

SIC Division	Original		>5 Million		>15 Million		>30 Million		Number of Observations Complete Case	% Change in Observation		
	Out (%)	Extreme Out (%)	Out (%)	Extreme Out (%)	Out (%)	Extreme Out (%)	Out (%)	Extreme Out (%)		>5 Million	>15 Million	>30 Million
Agriculture, Forestry, Fishing	8.95	3.5	7.59	2.95	6.48	2.31	7.41	2.65	257	−7.78	−15.95	−26.46
Finance, Insurance, and Real Estate	18.08	8.85	17.48	7.72	12.83	6.64	12.69	6.09	260	−5.38	−13.08	−24.23
Manufacturing, Materials, Machines, etc.	12.28	6.33	11.17	5.23	9.57	3.98	8.6	3.19	8,935	−6.11	−16.97	−29.11
Manufacturing, Food, Apparel, etc.	12.48	6.45	11.76	5.42	11.2	4.65	10.88	3.73	6,033	−4.54	−14.77	−26.26
Mining and Construction	10.4	4.24	9.78	3.82	9.1	3.47	8.74	3.26	2,289	−2.66	−9.31	−17.04
Transportation, Communication, Distribution	11.77	5.48	11.02	5	10.35	4.54	9.6	3.99	3,338	−2.37	−7.7	−16.72
Wholesale and Retail	8.29	3.19	8.02	2.77	7.77	2.5	7.92	2.19	3,788	−2.93	−9.32	−17.95
Other	14.07	6.87	13.62	6.11	12.94	5.66	11.55	4.81	9,613	−9.22	−25.13	−42.02

(continued)

Panel B: North American Dataset (Share of Outliers and Extreme for Different Size of Companies Determined by Total Assets)

SIC Division	Original Out (%)	Extreme (%)	>5 Million Out (%)	Extreme (%)	>15 Million Out (%)	Extreme (%)	>30 Million Out (%)	Extreme (%)	Number of Observation Complete Case	% Change in Observation >5 Million	>15 Million	>30 Million
Agriculture, Forestry, Fishing	9.06	3.4	10.33	2.89	8.84	3.26	8.78	2.93	265	-8.68	-18.87	-22.64
Finance,, Insurance, and Real Estate	12.46	5.63	11.68	5.03	10.99	4.17	10.63	3.35	1,272	-7.78	-22.72	-34.2
Manufacturing, Materials, Machines, etc.	11.34	5.1	11.09	4.77	9.82	3.74	9.19	3.33	17,653	-3.3	-12.74	-22.06
Manufacturing, Food, Apparel, etc.	13.16	6.42	12.74	5.91	11.62	5.24	10.94	4.6	9,038	-3.13	-10.84	-18.86
Mining and Construction	9.13	3.91	9.03	3.37	8.6	3.07	8.51	2.96	4,734	-4.06	-10.58	-17.32
Transportation, Communication, Distribution	14.73	6.06	14.49	5.97	13.9	5.33	13.29	4.75	5,821	-0.41	-2.63	-6.67
Wholesale and Retail	10.44	4.12	9.63	3.53	9.19	3.36	8.84	3.08	5,892	-1.87	-7.5	-12.88
Other	12.85	6.93	12.3	6.07	10.9	5.32	9.93	4.41	7,029	-5.24	-17.36	-28.62

The ">5 millions," ">15 millions," and ">30 millions" columns do not include observations whose total assets were less than 5, 15, and 30 million, respectively, with values deflated to the 1995 levels.

The "number of observations of complete case" indicates the total number of observations belonging to a given SIC division, for the complete case dataset.

Table 4.4. Needed Decrease in Share of Observations and Companies Per Industry to Make the ROA Distribution Normal.

Panel A.1. European Dataset (Skewness < 2; Kurtosis < 4)[a]

SIC Division	Skewness		Kurtosis		Companies		Observations		Change (%)	
	Treated	Complete	Treated	Complete	Treated	Complete	Treated	Complete	Companies	Observations
Agriculture, Forestry, Fishing	−1.02	−3.25	2.23	15	33	33	249	257	0	−3.11
Finance, Insurance, and Real Estate	−0.71	−1.93	3.83	7.29	34	36	242	260	−5.56	−6.92
Manufacturing, Materials, Machines, etc.	−1.77	−4.6	3.97	39.06	993	1,009	8,600	8,935	−1.59	−3.75
Manufacturing, Food, Apparel, etc.	−1.76	−3.54	3.98	20.24	677	688	5,805	6,033	−1.6	−3.78
Mining and Construction	−1.54	−9.11	3.94	129.21	257	259	2,217	2,289	−0.77	−3.15
Transportation, Communication, Distribution	−1.48	−8.77	3.99	149.75	397	409	3,184	3,338	−2.93	−4.61
Wholesale and Retail	−1.18	−4.33	3.98	36.67	438	442	3,660	3,788	−0.9	−3.38
Other	−1.74	−5.2	3.97	44.49	1,220	1,240	9,128	9,613	−1.61	−5.05

Panel A.2 European Dataset (Skewness < 0.5; Kurtosis <2)[a]

SIC Division	Skewness		Kurtosis		Companies		Observations		Change (%)	
	Treated	Complete	Treated	Complete	Treated	Complete	Treated	Complete	Companies	Observations
Agriculture, Forestry, Fishing	−0.4	−3.25	0.83	15	32	33	243	257	−3.03	−5.45
Finance, Insurance, and Real Estate	0.32	−1.93	1.72	7.29	34	36	233	260	−5.56	−10.38
Manufacturing, Materials, Machines, etc.	−0.5	−4.6	0.81	39.06	932	1,009	7,940	8,935	−7.63	−11.14
Manufacturing, Food, Apparel, etc.	−0.5	−3.54	0.74	20.24	648	688	5,349	6,033	−5.81	−11.34
Mining and Construction	−0.5	−9.11	0.82	129.21	254	259	2,118	2,289	−1.93	−7.47
Transportation, Communication, Distribution	−0.5	−8.77	1.31	149.75	432	442	3,616	3,788	−4.16	−7.85
Wholesale and Retail	−0.48	−4.33	1.5	36.67	1,163	1,240	8,407	9,613	−2.26	−4.54
Other	−0.5	−5.2	0.92	44.49	392	409	3,076	3,338	−6.21	−12.55

[a] The needed decrease in observations is determined by dropping the most extreme values until the kurtosis and skewness of the distribution are within the bounds of the normal distribution. We follow two different assumptions for "normal distribution," which generates two tables for each geographical region.

• The first normality assumption is determined by absolute values of skewness below 2 and excess kurtosis less than 4.

• The other normality assumption is determined by absolute values of skewness below 0.5 and kurtosis less than 2.

Panel B.1 North American Dataset (Skewness < 2; Kurtosis < 4)[a]

SIC Division	Skewness		Kurtosis		Companies		Observations		Change	
	Treated	Complete	Treated	Complete	Treated	Complete	Treated	Complete	Companies	Observations
Agriculture, Forestry, Fishing	-0.94	-4.66	2.32	41.08	24	26	259	265	-7.69	-2.26
Finance, Insurance, and Real Estate	-0.77	-11.2	3.7	224.14	147	148	1,230	1,272	-0.68	-3.3
Manufacturing, Materials, Machines, etc.	-1.56	-7.42	3.99	125.53	1,457	1,476	17,059	17,653	-1.29	-3.36
Manufacturing, Food, Apparel, etc.	-1.69	-6.34	3.98	75.58	758	766	8,623	9,038	-1.04	-4.59
Mining and Construction	-1.54	-30.5	3.88	1,462.45	499	503	4,605	4,734	-0.8	-2.72
Transportation, Communication, Distribution	-1.03	-20.98	3.94	832.09	497	506	5,563	5,821	-1.78	-4.43
Wholesale and Retail	-1.48	-6.22	3.89	80.42	558	571	5,700	5,892	-2.28	-3.26
Other	-1.77	-8.87	3.95	168.49	789	802	6,693	7,029	-1.62	-4.78

Panel B.2 North American Dataset (Skewness < 0.5; Kurtosis < 2)[a]

SIC Division	Skewness		Kurtosis		Companies		Observations		Change (%)	
	Treated	Complete	Treated	Complete	Treated	Complete	Treated	Complete	Companies	Observations
Agriculture, Forestry, Fishing	−0.45	−4.66	0.89	41.08	23	26	251	265	−11.54	−5.28
Finance, Insurance, and Real Estate	−0.26	−11.2	1.96	224.14	146	148	1,203	1,272	−1.35	−5.42
Manufacturing, Materials, Machines, etc.	−0.5	−7.42	0.75	125.53	1,429	1,476	16,068	17,653	−3.18	−8.98
Manufacturing, Food, Apparel, etc.	−0.5	−6.34	0.96	75.58	727	766	8,060	9,038	−5.09	−10.82
Mining and Construction	−0.5	−30.5	0.64	1,462.45	494	503	4,406	4,734	−1.79	−6.93
Transportation, Communication, Distribution	−0.5	−20.98	1.92	832.09	488	506	5,377	5,821	−3.56	−7.63
Wholesale and Retail	−0.5	−6.22	1.02	80.42	543	571	5,500	5,892	−4.9	−6.65
Other	−0.5	−8.87	0.69	168.49	759	802	6,124	7,029	−5.36	−12.88

[a] The needed decrease in observations is determined by dropping the most extreme values until the kurtosis and skewness of the distribution are within the bounds of the normal distribution. We follow two different assumptions for "normal distribution," which generates two tables for each geographical region.

• The first normality assumption is determined by absolute values of skewness below 2 and excess kurtosis less than 4.

• The other normality assumption is determined by absolute values of skewness below 0.5 and kurtosis less than 2.

European dataset, it was necessary to drop an average of 4.2% of the observations to have a normal distribution across each of the SIC Divisions. In the North American dataset (Panel B.1) it would be necessary to drop around 3.8% in average of the observations to satisfy the looser normality criteria. If, on the other hand, the narrower more stringent definition of normality was followed, then it would be necessary to drop an average of 9% of the observations in the European dataset (Panel A.2). By comparison, it would be necessary to drop around 8% of all observations on average across industries to reach normality in the North American dataset (Panel B.2).

However, the calculations show great variations across the various SIC Divisions in terms of the required share of companies and observations to be dropped. For example, in the European dataset Finance Insurance and Real Estate, Manufacturing Materials Machines, Manufacturing Food Apparel and Other industries would need to drop more than 10% of the total observations to reach normality whereas the Wholesale and Retail sectors only needed to drop 4.5% of the sampled firms. The North American dataset shows less variation compared to the European dataset, although the SIC Division of Manufacturing Food Apparel needed to drop the most observations to reach at normality exceeding 10% of the total observations, almost double of the 5.3% of observations dropped in Agriculture, Forestry, and Fishing.

Concluding Notes

The preceding analyses show that the outlier phenomenon is pervasive where quite a substantial proportion of the collected data must be dropped in order to satisfy the common criteria for a normal distribution of performance outcomes measured by financial return (ROA). These analyses are based on data following the complete case approach, which means that the number of observations dropped from the original dataset for us to have a normal distribution most likely is even higher and significantly so.

This suggests that simple assumptions about normality in observed performance data often are wrong and ignores the (often) substantial number of outliers that exist in the samples even after various cutoff techniques have been applied to gain normality like data conditions.

However, the pervasiveness of outliers as reflected in substantial excess kurtosis and (extreme) negative skewness in the performance distributions call for further and more detailed studies to examine the underlying distribution of the performance data.

References

Schwertman, N. C., Owens, M. A., & Adnan, R. (2004). A simple more general Boxplot method for identifying outliers. *Computational Statistics & Data Analysis, 47*(1), 165–174.
Tukey, J. W. (1977). *Exploratory data analysis*. Boston, MA: Addison-Wesley.

Chapter 5

Background and Prior Studies

Abstract

This chapter introduces empirical studies of firm performance and related
risk outcomes conducted in the management and finance fields presenting underlying theoretical rationales as they have evolved over time. Early
finance studies of market-based returns predominantly found positively
skewed return distributions that conform to assumptions about higher
returns associated with more risky investments. Subsequent studies found
that performance outcomes measured as accounting-based financial returns
generally display left-skewed distributions that reflect negative risk-return
relationships. This artifact was first observed by Bowman (1980), thus
often referred to as the "Bowman paradox" because it contravened the
conventional assumptions in finance. The management studies have largely
confirmed the inverse risk-return observations but often following rather
confined research streams. A contingency perspective inspired by prospect
theory and behavioral rationales have investigated the lagged effects of performance on risk outcomes and *vice versa*. Another stream has focused on
the spurious relationships between negatively skewed performance distributions and the inverse risk-return associations. A third approach considered
the performance and risk outcomes as deriving from the firms responding in
distinct ways to exogenous changes. These studies reach comparable results
but underpinned by very different rationales. The finance studies observe
deviations from the pure doctrine of positive risk-return associations embedded in the widely adopted capital asset pricing model (CAPM) and note
deficiencies with alternative interpretations that even question the validity
of CAPM. A more recent strain of studies in behavioral finance observes
how many (even professional) investment managers have biases that lead
to inverse relationships between perceived risk and return outcomes. While
these diverse fields of study have different starting points, they uncover an

A Study of Risky Business Outcomes: Adapting to Strategic Disruption, 67–82
Copyright © 2023 by Torben Juul Andersen
Published under exclusive licence by Emerald Publishing Limited
doi:10.1108/978-1-83797-074-220231005

increasing number of interesting commonalities that can inspire the ongoing search for explanations to observed left-skewed financial returns and negative risk-return correlations across firms.

Keywords: Adaptation; behavioral theory of the firm; cognitive biases; overconfidence; prospect theory; strategic response capabilities

Introduction

As observed from the performance data analyzed in the previous chapters, the distribution of financial returns (ROA) and other comparable indicators show distributions characterized by high negative skewness and substantive positive excess kurtosis that fail to comply with the common assumptions about normally distributed outcomes. In short, the prevalence of outliers, particularly among low performers in the (negative) left tail is a very notable and regularly featured phenomenon.

Various studies consistently observe left-skewed distributions of financial returns with (extreme) tails of poor performers and some superior firms in a narrow positive tail (e.g., Albæk & Andersen, 2021; Alfarano, Milaković, Irle, & Kauschke, 2012; Williams, Baek, Park, & Zhao, 2016). This phenomenon is systematically displayed in empirical studies where associated outliers typically are eliminated from the sample to justify convenient assumptions of normality that disregard and thus avoid closer examination of outliers in mainstream management research (Boisot & McKelvey, 2011; Taleb, 2007, 2013). However, further studies of real-world data may provide a deeper understanding of the left-skewed performance distributions and generate important insights about the underlying dynamics of the outlying organizations that constitute the phenomenon.

That is, the performance distributions of firms are often negatively skewed with (extreme) negative outliers in the left tails but we typically cannot, or do not devote much effort to explain this commonly observed phenomenon. Organizational and management studies typically investigate modeled relationships based on the statistical significance of mean-value relationships determined in ordinary least-square regressions and similar statistical analytical methods even though the outcome variables may have leptokurtic characteristics in violation of assumed Gaussian properties. Risky, or (highly) uncertain business environments with abrupt and unexpected events that disrupt prevailing strategies and make the status quo untenable, increase the need to respond to impending changes and adapt organizational activities accordingly. Emerging conditions of different types of extreme disaster-like losses will increasingly challenge the common assumption about normally distributed outcome effects (e.g., Kunreuther & Useem, 2018; McKelvey & Andriani, 2005; Nordhaus, 2011; Taleb, 2005, 2007). Hence, it is observed how underperforming firms are more vulnerable to extreme environmental changes and lead to left-skewed performance outcomes with negative risk-return relations (e.g., Becerra & Markarian, 2021). These abnormal performers may include firms that engage in capital-intensive research and development efforts to advance their future business acumen. Yet, we rarely examine these representative organizations even though they provide opportunities to gain deeper insights about the business dynamics that may help explain the prevalence of left-skewed performance tails.

A number of empirical studies have uncovered associations between left-skewed performance distributions (negative skewness) and negative relationships between average performance and performance risk measured as standard deviation in outcomes (e.g., Henkel, 2000, 2009; Lustig & Verdelhan, 2012; Ruefli, 1990). In the strategy field, the negative risk-return phenomenon using accounting-based performance measures have been reported for a long time and is often referred to as the "Bowman paradox" in honor of the first scholar to report these intriguing results (Bowman, 1980; Nickel & Rodriguez, 2002). They contravene common assumptions in the finance field. Finance theory typically associates lower yields to risk-free financial assets like treasuries compared to returns awarded to, say, risk-ridden corporate junk bonds thereby assuming a positive relationship between perceived risk and expected returns. This assumption is also reflected in the CAPM that stipulates a positive relationship between the beta of a stock that expresses the correlation between the stock price and systematic market changes (e.g., Sharpe, 1964). So, the "Bowman's paradox" provoked a common belief at least as it was initially presented. However, subsequent empirical studies in finance have challenged the premises of CAPM and eventually failed to confirm the positive relationship between stock returns and market risk (e.g., Fama & French, 1992).

The finance field has typically adopted market-based returns as the relevant performance measure and captured the related level of risk by the standard deviation in the stock price, or derived market returns. The strategy and management fields typically apply accounting-based returns as the relevant performance measures often expressed as a relative ratio, such as, net income as a percentage of total assets referred to as return on assets (ROA). Finance studies have often found positively skewed distributions of market returns that support the assertion of a positive relationship between risk and return. However, several more recent studies have been less categorical and have reported partially negative, or insignificant positive risk-return relations. Management studies have quite consistently reported negatively skewed return distributions with negative risk-return relationships using accounting-based return measures. Apart from adopting different return measures, market-based versus accounting-based, these performance measures project different time perspectives where finance in fact assess *ex ante* relationships looking at expected returns and risk levels whereas management conducts *ex post* analyses of realized and reported results.

In corporate finance, the systematic risk is expressed in the stock beta that indicates how the stock price is expected to respond to changes in the general market value, whereas price changes beyond this is ascribed to unsystematic firm-specific factors, that in principle can be eliminated in a diversified investment portfolio of listed stocks. This means that mainstream finance for a long period of time considered unsystematic risk as being irrelevant, which presented a conundrum because strategy scholars perceive the firm-specific conditions and risks as very central aspects of strategic management that can help us understand why some firms overperform while others underperform (Bettis, 1983). In the strategy field, the ability to identify and deal with idiosyncratic organizational risks and strategic threats reflect responsive organizational processes that generate renewal in support of needed adaptive moves (e.g., Adner & Helfat, 2003; Bettis & Hitt, 1995; Teece, Pisano, & Shuen, 1997). Parts of the finance field has subsequently relaxed some of the market-based assumptions supporting rationales for value creation through effective management of firm-specific risk as it can help generate steady internal cash flows for positive investments (Froot, Scharfstein, & Stein, 1993). It may also reduce the risk of default and costly bankruptcy (Stulz, 1996) as well as systematic risk management processes can increase efficiency through coordinated handling of corporate exposures (e.g., Bartram, 2000; Nocco & Stulz, 2006).

Theoretical Underpinnings

As appears from the initial presentation of the topic, the fields of management and finance adopt quite different views in the assessment of firm performance and the eventual distribution of performance outcomes. Management scholars typically analyze many diverse aspects of the organizational dynamic including effects of leadership, elements of organizational structure, behavioral and cultural aspects. In contrast, finance scholars have typically focused on firm effects in financial markets that trade different debt instruments including corporate stocks where the behavior and expectations of investors will affect the market-based performance outcomes. By extension, the analysis to inform corporate investment decisions, that obviously resemble strategic decisions by (potentially) committing substantial resources into new project ventures that will define the future realized business outcomes, typically adopt the CAPM-rationales as applied in discounted cash flow (DCF) methodologies. Despite these rather fundamental differences in perspective, we can observe an increasing confluence in the empirical evidence on the observed risk-return relationships uncovered in newer studies within the two disciplines, or fields of study.

The following outlines some of the common approaches adopted by scholars in the management field when they study the performance outcomes across firms, and assess the cross-sectional and longitudinal relationships between risk and performance, and *vice versa*. We also attempt to outline some of the key findings uncovered in various empirical studies in the finance field based on different data-driven analytical approaches using both historical market information as well as behavior-related information with individual assessments assembled from real investment managers. This examination reveals some seemingly common characteristics with an interesting evolving confluence in empirical findings that we try to interpret without any claims of reaching a final consensus.

Management Studies

The management field has typically been studying the observed left-skewed distributions of accounting-based performance ratios with negative risk-return relationships from three rather distinct theoretical vantage points. The first approach has typically studied the risk-return relationships as contingencies where one affects the outcomes of the other, and *vice versa*, possibly also conceived as simultaneous relationships. The second approach considers the observed phenomena as the effect of partially spurious relationships between interlinked statistical measures of mean values and their standard deviations. The third approach looks at the observed phenomena as the outcome of heterogeneous adaptive strategy-making processes applied across competing firms in various industry settings. While there are some overlaps between the three approaches, they often appear to constitute and follow rather separate research streams as manifested over time.

The "Bowman paradox" originates from Bowman's (1980) study where his analyses showed that many firms operating across different industries showed a link between higher after-tax profit over equity (ROE) and lower levels of risk indicated by the variance in ROE. Other studies associated the phenomenon identified by the competitive conditions in specific industry contexts as affecting the performance outcomes expressed in associated risk and return measures (Cool & Schendel, 1988). That is, the intensity of competition and the relative market power of firms was found to influence the risk-return outcomes (Cool, Dierickx, & Jemison, 1989). In analyses of the relationships between lagged measures of *ex ante* performance forecasts by financial analysts and the variation in forecasts as a risk indicator, Bromiley (1991) uncovered negative relationships between risk and expected returns and *vice versa*. Using very different performance indicators derived from lending decisions by bankers McNamara and Bromiley (1997, 1999) identified comparable inverse risk-return relationships. More recently, Santacruz (2019) reproduced the negative relationships between risk and returns based on various alternative risk-taking indicators from among a list of alternative financial ratios. Hence, the negative risk-return relationship is rather well documented in a large number of studies conducted over the past decades.

A common way to explain the inverse risk-return relationships is that decision-makers react stronger to losses than to equivalent gains in line with prospect theory (Kahnemann & Tversky, 1979) and the behavioral theory of the firm (Cyert & March, 1963). So, Bowman (1982) early on observed that troubled companies seem to assume larger risks as a way to improve on bad performance as a possible explanation for the negative association between return and risk. It could be reasoned that a positive frame where the firm is performing well with high levels of return cause executive decision-makers to be more risk-averse whereas a negative frame with poor performance and low returns lead decision-makers to seek more risk (e.g., Bazerman, 1984). Some studies found less-than-acceptable performance levels to have a negative relationship to risk dependent on the level of organizational slack available and the decision structure adopted by the organization (e.g., Singh, 1986). Studies consistently found negative relations between risk and return relationships among firms performing below their target and positive relations among firms performing above target (e.g., Fiegenbaum, 1990; Fiegenbaum & Thomas, 1988). Many other studies have reproduced similar, or comparable results across different industrial settings (e.g., Jegers, 1991; Johnson, 1992; Sinha, 1994; Wiseman & Catanach, 1997; Wiseman & Gomez-Mejia, 1998). The behavioral factors ascribed to executives have been uncovered in studies of failed companies where dysfunctional leadership leads to risky actions and poor business execution that explain their inability to respond to market changes that eventually leads to bankruptcy (e.g., Herracleus & Werres, 2016). Narcissistic traits and overconfidence of executive decision-makers can induce risk-taking behaviors where compensation schemes and incentives in the form of stock options may enforce them (e.g., Buyl, Boone, & Wade, 2019). Hence, overconfident decision-makers that commit to large (public) project investments seem to trigger major cost overruns and underperforming project outcomes (Flyvbjerg & Bester, 2021) often induced by political biases where the decision-makers deliberately try to distort the analyses and oversell their (prestige) projects (e.g., Flyvbjerg, 2021).

Some studies have uncovered the negative risk-return relationships from ordinary least-square regressions whereas the results have been absent in more advanced two- or three-stage regression analyses that consider potential endogeneity effects associated with the implied two-way model relations (e.g., Bettis, 1982; Oviatt & Bauerschmidt, 1991). This might suggest that significant relationships found in the conventional empirical studies are caused by, or are at least partially affected by miss-specified models, simplified methodologies, or insufficient measures. Accordingly, some researchers explain the negative risk-return relationships as the outcome of statistical artifacts linked to the way the return and risk measures are specified as related statistical measures derived from the same time-bound dataset. Hence, it argued that the relationships between mean values and the associated variance, or standard deviation of a given dataset cannot be verified as a general relationship because the two measures are arithmetically derived from the same specific datasets (Ruefli, 1990). It is further argued that even if the distribution is normal and stable, a significant number of firms in the dataset will typically impose spurious effects on the calculated risk-return relationships, which makes the use of simple mean variance approaches in empirical studies very problematic (e.g., Ruefli, 1991; Ruefli & Wiggins, 1994; Ruefli, Collins, & Lacugna, 1999). Henkel (2000) found that negatively skewed distributions automatically generate negative mean and variance relationships and in a later study, he isolated the spurious elements in the inverse risk-return correlations of negatively skewed return distributions showing that they can generate a substantial part of the calculated inverse risk-return relationships (Henkel, 2009).

An alternative explanation was offered early on for the observed inverse risk-return relationships, namely the possible effects of "good management" where effective executive decisions simultaneously improve profitability and reduce discrepancies in performance (Bowman, 1980). In strategic management this is expressed as potential effects of adaptive responses, or strategic response capabilities depicting an ability to react fast and effectively to surprising changes (Bettis & Hitt, 1995). This in many ways resembles the concept of "dynamic capabilities" defined as an "ability to integrate, build, and reconfigure internal and external competences to address rapidly changing environments" (Teece, Pisano, & Shuen, 1997, p. 516). It is arguably reflected in organizational processes to sense the changing environment, seize emerging opportunities, and restructure activities to adapt (Teece, 2007). This quality has also been associated with (dynamic) managerial capabilities "with which managers build, integrate, and reconfigure organizational resources and competences" (Adner & Helfat, 2003, p. 1012) explicating how managers engage to adjust and adapt business activities in tune with changes in the surrounding environment (Helfat & Martin, 2015). The ability to handle disruptive risk events effectively has been found associated with lower adjustment costs and higher operating efficiencies that create value for the firm (Miller & Chen, 2003). This improved ability to deal with emergent risk events and adapt the business activities accordingly can make the firm a more reliable counterpart, which may harness important and valuable stakeholder relationships as a way to sustain competitive advantage (Wang, Barney, & Reuer, 2003).

A certain randomness in organizational processes can differentiate performance outcomes and create persistent differences in firm profitability where skewed and serially correlated financial returns will be associated with negative risk-return relations (Denrell, 2004). For example, if competing firms adapt in different ways by reducing their poorly performing activities, that dynamic can generate U-shaped relationships between risk and return where low performers show negative risk-return relationships and high performers positive risk-return relations (Denrell, 2008). This can be modeled as a dynamic strategic responsiveness process where competing firms in a given industry context attempt to adapt activities in view of observed market changes thereby gaining a better strategic fit with the environmental conditions at any point in time. Assuming that a good strategic fit leads to higher performance outcomes, for example, as satisfied customers demand more goods and generate higher revenues while use of efficient technologies reduce costs, the ability to respond effectively will generate higher and less and volatile performance levels (Andersen, Denrell, & Bettis, 2007). In other words, effective strategic responsiveness will be associated with a negative relationship between average performance and the standard deviation in performance over given time intervals. Hence, one can argue that corporate leaders, or managers can orchestrate adaptive moves through effective response capabilities what will generate higher returns at lower risk levels (Andersen, 2015, 2021).

This approach to analyze risk-return effects take on a particular meaning when we add some newer emerging perspectives to the interpretation of environmental conditions and the way they evolve as businesses and firms attempt to deal with them. We seem to observe increasingly disruptive business conditions where risk events emerge with little prior warning and take firms by surprise where the preceding developments happen in subtle and unpredictable ways. One interpretation of this evolving context is that it may lead to major loss effects that create negatively skewed performance outcomes across a wider sample of firms. These contexts are often considered highly complex and affected by stochastic non-linear path-dependent and irreversible actions that (often) lead to non-Gaussian outcomes with (potentially) extreme effects (Nicolis & Prigogine, 1989;

Prigogine, 1987). It represents a competitive landscape where rapid technological innovation leads to disruptive and (often) unpredictable changes (e.g., Bettis & Hitt, 1995). Hence, the potential impact of random occurrences and circumstances are typically underestimated where the possibility of unexpected events are ignored (Taleb, 2005, 2007). As we attempt to analyze the effects of these phenomena based on Gaussian statistical methods, we consequently overlook and inadvertently disregard effects of abrupt disruptive discontinuities (Mandelbrot & Taleb, 2006). That is, analyses published in mainstream management journals that assume a Gaussian distribution across independent data observations will not conceive of extreme events that do arise from time to time and impose disproportionately high costs on businesses and the societies they operate in (Baum & McKelvey, 2006; Boisot & McKelvey, 2011). The high-impact low-probability events associated with highly erratic and unpredictable environments can impose high cost and losses on operational activities where conventional statistical analyses fail to adequately capture and account for these phenomena (Nordhaus, 2011). It is in this context, that poorly performing firms may become particularly vulnerable to impending abrupt changes, or disruptive shocks as a particular dynamic that enforces the negative risk-return relations (e.g., Becerra & Markarian, 2021).

Finance Studies

The finance field typically uses market-based returns to capture firm performance with related risk effects expressed as the standard deviation in the firm's stock returns. Many of the early studies found return distributions with positive skewness indicating a positive risk-return relation although more recent studies have uncovered non-existent or partially negative risk-return relationships. Management studies typically use accounting-based return measures, for example, ROA, where the evidence quite consistently displays negatively skewed return distributions with negative relationships between measures of risk and return. While studies in the management field typically display negative risk-return relationships based on the accounting-based performance measures, it should be noted that this relationship seems to disappear when market-based returns are adopted as measures of performance (e.g., Fiegenbaum & Thomas, 1986). So, the findings are seemingly consistent although based on different premises. Given the application of different performance measures, the finance approach reflects an *ex ante* perspective on the relationship between perceived risk and expected returns whereas management (typically) adopts an *ex post* perspective and analyses the relationship between realized performance and risk outcomes as reported in the corporate accounts.

Finance studies typically analyze the distribution of market-based returns from public-listed firms traded on (presumed) liquid stock exchanges. The CAPM reflects an early interpretation of the associated risk-return relationships and this model continues to be applied in present-day corporate finance practice. The basic argument is that market conditions for financial assets traded on liquid exchanges consistently fall along a capital market line with a positive relationship between the perceived risk of the stock and the return it provides in addition to the risk-free rate (Sharpe, 1964). This premium is expected to reflect the beta of the stock capturing the degree of covariation between the stock price and the general market index, that is, the systematic risk.

Early analyses of market-based returns found standard deviation and skewness of returns to provide fair descriptions of perceived risk (e.g., Fisher & Hall, 1969) although it could be argued that a simple relationship between two factors like mean and variance of returns in fact is a generalization of the relationships adopted in the prior investment decisions (Fama, 1971). However, market-based returns display both positive and negative skewness, although positively skewed distributions appear to be more prevalent, which could suggest two combined distributions with above mean returns following one distribution whereas below mean returns are drawn from another different distribution (Simkowitz & Beedles, 1980). Later studies have found positively skewed stock returns but also observed that a positively skewed distribution is a poor predictor of distribution skewness in subsequent periods thus hinting that abnormal returns above the mean is unstable and might follow an inverse development (Singleton & Wingender, 1986).

The stock price developments display a certain inertia where they (only) slowly revert toward their mean value (potentially) drifting away from the central tendency for longer periods of time. Such time-bound movements in stock prices can create negative autocorrelations between returns at different times over longer holding periods thus hinting that negative returns can lead to subsequent positive returns and the other way around (Fama & French, 1988). Increasing volatility of the stock price development was observed to raise the required rate of return by lowering stock prices, which may explain a negatively skewed return distribution with excess kurtosis (Campbell & Hentschel, 1992).

In a seminal study, Fama and French (1992) failed to find that the stock beta had a relationship to stock returns as prescribed by the CAPM showing instead that the ratio of book over market value is a better predictor of future returns. It was also found that the reversion of stock prices toward their mean value differs according to performance levels where faster reversion toward the mean happens when stock returns are below the mean or are far from the mean both above and below (Fama & French, 2000).

Later studies found different return characteristics across asset classes with negatively skewed returns more prevalent in stocks of small companies compared to large stock indices (e.g., Alles & Kling, 1994). The price volatility of individual stocks was found to increase after major stock price drops suggesting that some return elements are positively skewed while other market-related effects impose negatively skewed returns (Duffee, 1995). The negative skew in stock returns were found to be associated with disclosure of new information and particularly pronounced when stock options are part of the executive compensation package (Ekholm & Pasternack, 2005). Analyses of risk-neutral return distributions uncover negative relations between the stock price volatility and the subsequent market returns on the stock with a positive association to the kurtosis of the return distribution (e.g., Conrad, Dittmar, & Ghysels, 2013).

The firm returns are found to be unbalanced with leptokurtosis being higher for returns below the mode among firms that turn out to have relatively shorter life spans (Dichev, Graham, Harvey, & Rajgopal, 2013). So, variation in returns appear to be higher among lower performing firms hinting an inverse risk-return relationship among short-lived firms. The "extreme" return distributions are confirmed in other studies, for example, Tobin's q (a market-based performance indicator) appears to follow an asymmetric Laplace distribution (Scharfenaker & dos Santos, 2015) and stock returns are found to resemble a leptokurtic Cauchy distribution (Williams, Baek, Park, & Zhao, 2016). Hence, the extant literature generally confirms the non-Gaussian contours of performance distributions.

The negative risk-return relationship has also been analyzed from a behavioral perspective as individual investors may have personal biases that lead to inefficient price assessments of the financial assets (Shefrin, 2007). The issue seems to be that a substantial number of investors expect that larger (successful) firms (by implication) will generate higher future returns as reflective of past successful growth, which also generates a bias in their risk assessment. Hence, a substantial number of (even professional) investors will automatically associate long-term value with the size of the firm and its market-to-book ratio. This association between expected return and assumed volatility of the stock price ascribes higher returns and lower risk to large firm stocks, so perceived risk has a negative relationship to expected returns (Shefrin, 2014, 2016).

The insights derived from studying parts of the prior management and finance literatures on performance distributions and associated risk outcomes have been summarized and listed to enable contrasting and comparative evaluations (Table 5.1). To this end, we note different starting points with distinct foci on individual firm characteristics in management and (stock) market characteristics in finance. Yet, despite the different perspectives assumed in the two fields of study, we notice common empirical findings that point toward influences of firm-specific traits, for example, expressed as size and leadership effects that eventually produce non-normal leptokurtic return distributions. The theoretical rationales and methodological approaches differ, but nonetheless uncover some strikingly compatible findings, such as, failure to argue for "simple" direct risk-return relations, showing value from active responses to deal with risk events, and pinpointing the importance of behavior.

As appears from these empirical snapshots extracted from various management and finance studies published over the past decades, the (often) automatic assumptions about simple relationships between risk and return are increasingly being questioned paving the way for more nuanced considerations. The empirical evidence generally uncovers non-normal leptokurtic return distributions (often) with negative tails and inverse risk-return relations linked to specific market conditions, industry features, firm attributes, individual (investor) biases, and various leadership, or managerial artifacts.

Table 5.1. Comparing Performance and Risk-Return Studies in Management and Finance.

	Management Studies	Finance Studies
The performance distribution	• Firm-specific conditions are key to explain performance (Bettis, 1983) • Competitive conditions affect performance and risk outcomes (Cool & Schendel, 1988; Cool, Dierickx, & Jemison, 1989) • The impact of random events is underestimated (Taleb, 2005, 2007) • High-impact low-probability events impose higher operational costs and extraordinary losses (Nordhaus, 2011) • Vulnerability to extreme events can cause left-skewed returns and negative risk-return relations (Becerra & Markarian, 2021)	• Different distributions for above and below mean returns (Simkowitz & Beedles, 1980) • Volatility raises the required return and lowers prices to cause negatively skewed returns (Campbell & Hentschel, 1992) • Negatively skewed returns are prevalent in small stock indices (Alles & Kling, 1994) • Negative skewness in returns is linked to new disclosure and executive stock options (Ekholm & Pasternack, 2005) • Stock returns resemble a leptokurtic Cauchy distribution (Williams, Baek, Park, & Zhao, 2016)
The risk-return relationship	*Contingencies* • Firms assume larger risks to improve bad performance (Bowman, 1982) • Negative relationships between risk and expected returns (Bromiley, 1991; McNamara & Bromiley, 1997, 1999) • Negative relationships between risk and realized returns (Santacruz, 2019)	*Required return* • There is a positive relationship between the stock return and the systematic market risk (Sharpe, 1964) • Fail to reproduce the positive relationship between stock returns and market risk (Fama & French, 1992) • Positive skewness is a poor predictor of subsequent skewness and might develop inversely (Singleton & Wingender, 1986)

(continued)

Table 5.1.   Comparing Performance and Risk-Return Studies in Management and Finance. (Continued)

	Management Studies	Finance Studies
The risk-return relationship	*Spurious effects* • Mean variance calculations are arithmetically linked and cannot be verified (Ruefli, 1990) • Some firm data will cause spurious effects in the risk-return calculations (Ruefli & Wiggins, 1994; Ruefli, Collins, & Lacugna, 1999) • Negatively skewed distributions are associated with inverse risk-returns (Henkel, 2000, 2009) *Response processes* • Good managers can increase profits and reduce performance discrepancies at the same time (Bowman, 1980) • The ability to react fast to surprises enhances competitiveness (Bettis & Hitt, 1995) • Managing disruptive events reduces adjustment costs (Miller & Chen, 2003) • Random processes can create negative risk-return relations (Denrell, 2004) • Effective responses can generate higher and less volatile performance outcomes (Andersen, Denrell, & Bettis, 2007) • Overconfidence can induce unprofitable risk-taking behaviors (Buyl, Boone, & Wade, 2019)	• Negative autocorrelations between returns over different time periods (Fama & French, 1988) • A negative relationship between price volatility and subsequent market returns (Conrad, Dittmar, & Ghysels, 2013) *Risk management* • Effective risk management makes free cash available for value-creating investments (Froot, Scharfstein, & Stein, 1993) • Risk management efforts can reduce default and bankruptcy costs (Stulz, 1996) • Systematic risk management avoids excessive losses and increases efficiency (Bartram, 2000; Nocco & Stulz, 2006) *Behavioral biases* • Individual investor biases can lead to inefficient assessments of financial asset prices (Shefrin, 2007) • Professional investors can have a bias that links perceived risk to lower returns (Shefrin, 2014, 2016)

Conclusion

The preceding overview of prior studies that examine the distribution of firm performance and associated relationships to performance risk pursued in different research streams within the distinct management and finance fields show evidence of left-skewed returns and inverse risk-return relationships. Despite some distinct differences in theoretical foundation and methodological approaches in these diverse fields of study, we also discern some commonalities in the empirical evidence.

In the next chapter, we will take a closer look at performance distributions and risk-return relationships among firms that operate in different manufacturing industries and assess possible links to different managerial artifacts.

References

Adner, R., & Helfat, C. (2003). Corporate effects and dynamic managerial capabilities. *Strategic Management Journal, 24*(10), 1011–1025.

Albæk, M., & Andersen, T. J. (2021). The distribution of performance data: Consistent evidence of (extreme) negative outcomes. In T. J. Andersen (Ed.), *Strategic responsiveness for a sustainable future: New research international management* (pp. 147–174). Bingley: Emerald Publishing.

Alfarano, S., Milaković, M., Irle, A., & Kauschke, J. (2012). A statistical equilibrium model of competitive firms. *Journal of Economic Dynamics & Control, 36*, 136–149.

Alles, L. A., & Kling, J. L. (1994). Regularities in the variation of skewness in asset returns. *Journal of Financial Research, 17*(3), 427–438.

Andersen, T. J. (2015). Interactive strategy-making: Combining central reasoning with ongoing learning from decentralised responses. *Journal of General Management, 40*(4), 69–88.

Andersen, T. J. (2021). Dynamic adaptive strategy-making processes for enhanced strategic responsiveness. In T. J. Andersen (Ed.), *Strategic responses for a sustainable future: New research in international management* (pp. 49–65). Bingley: Emerald Publishing.

Andersen, T. J., Denrell, J., & Bettis, R. A. (2007). Strategic responsiveness and Bowman's risk-return paradox. *Strategic Management Journal, 28*, 407–429.

Bartram, S. M. (2000). Corporate risk management as a lever for shareholder value creation. *Financial Markets, Institutions and Instruments, 9*, 279–324.

Baum, J. A., & McKelvey, B. (2006). Analysis of extremes in management studies. In D. J. Ketchen & D. D. Bergh (Eds.), *Research methodology in strategy and management – Volume 3* (pp. 123–196). Bingley: Emerald Publishing.

Bazerman, M. H. (1984). The relevance of Kahneman and Tversky's concept of framing to organizational behavior. *Journal of Management, 10*, 333–343.

Becerra, M., & Markarian, G. (2021). Why are firms with lower performance more volatile and unpredictable? A vulnerability explanation of the Bowman paradox. *Organization Science, 32*(5), 1327–1345.

Bettis, R. A. (1982). Risk considerations in modeling corporate strategy. *Academy of Management Proceedings, 1982*(1), 22–25.

Bettis, R. A. (1983). Modern financial theory, corporate strategy and public policy: Three conundrums. *Academy of Management Review, 8*(3), 406–415.

Bettis, R. A., & Hitt, M. A. (1995). The new competitive landscape. *Strategic Management Journal, 16*, 7–19.

Boisot, M., & McKelvey, B. (2011). Connectivity, extremes, and adaptation: A power-law perspective of organizational effectiveness. *Journal of Management Inquiry, 20*(2), 119–133.

Bowman, E. H. (1980). A risk–return paradox for strategic management. *Sloan Management Review, 21*(3), 17–31.

Bowman, E. H. (1982). Risk seeking by troubled firms. *Sloan Management Review, 23*, 33–43.

Bromiley, P. (1991). Testing a causal model of corporate risk taking and performance. *Academy of Management Journal, 34*(1), 37–59.

Buyl, T., Boone, C., & Wade, J. B. (2019). CEO narcissism, risk-taking, and resilience: An empirical analysis in U.S. commercial banks. *Journal of Management, 45*(4), 1372–1400.

Campbell, J. Y., & Hentschel, L. (1992). No news is good news: An asymmetric model of changing volatility in stock returns. *Journal of Financial Economics, 31*, 281–318.

Conrad, J., Dittmar, R. F., & Ghysels, E. (2013). Ex ante skewness and expected stock returns. *Journal of Finance, 68*(1), 85–124.

Cool, K., Dierickx, I., & Jamison, D. (1989). Business strategy, market structure and risk-return relationships: A structural approach. *Strategic Management Journal, 10*(6), 507–522.

Cool, K., & Schendel, D. (1988). Performance differences among strategic group members. *Strategic Management Journal, 9*(3), 207–223.

Cyert, R. M., & March, J. G. (1963). *A behavioral theory of the firm*. Hoboken, NJ: Prentice Hall.

Denrell, J. (2004). Random walks and sustained competitive advantage. *Management Science, 50*(7), 922–934.

Denrell, J. (2008). Organizational risk taking: Adaptation versus variable risk preferences. *Industrial and Corporate Change, 17*(3), 427–466.

Dichev, I. D., Graham, J. R., Harvey, C. R., & Rajgopal, S. (2013). Earnings quality: Evidence from the field. *Journal of Accounting and Economics, 56*, 1–33.

Duffee, G. R. (1995). Stock returns and volatility: A firm-level analysis. *Journal of Financial Economics, 37*, 399–420.

Ekholm, A., & Pasternack, D. (2005). The negative news threshold: An explanation for negative skewness in stock returns. *European Journal of Finance, 11*(6), 511–529.

Fama, E. F. (1971). Risk, return, and equilibrium. *Journal of Political Economy, 79*(1), 30–55.

Fama, E. F., & French, K. R. (1988). Permanent and temporary components of stock prices. *Journal of Political Economy, 96*(2), 246–273.

Fama, E. F., & French, K. R. (1992). The cross section of expected stock returns. *Journal of Finance, 47*, 427–465.

Fama, E. F., & French, K. R. (2000). Forecasting profitability and earnings. *Journal of Business, 73*(2), 161–175.

Fiegenbaum, A. (1990). Prospect theory and the risk-return association: An empirical examination in 85 industries. *Journal of Economic Behavior and Organization, 14*, 187–203.

Fiegenbaum, A., & Thomas, H. (1986). Dynamic and risk measurement perspectives on Bowman's risk-return paradox for strategic management: An empirical study. *Strategic Management Journal, 7*, 395–407.

Fiegenbaum, A., & Thomas, H. (1988). Attitudes toward risk and the risk-return paradox: Prospect theory explanations. *Academy of Management Journal, 31*, 85–106.

Fisher, I. N., & Hall, G. R. (1969). Risk and corporate rates of return. *The Quarterly Journal of Economics, 83*(1), 79–92.

Flyvbjerg, B. (2021). Top ten behavioral biases in project management: An overview. *Project Management Journal, 52*(6), 531–546.

Flyvbjerg, B., & Bester, D. W. (2021). The cost-benefit fallacy: Why cost-benefit analysis is broken and how to fix it. *Journal of Benefit Cost Analysis, 12*(3), 395–419.

Froot, K., Scharfstein, D., & Stein J. (1993). Risk management: coordinating corporate investment and financing policies. *Journal of Finance, 48*(5), 1629–1658.

Helfat, C. E., & Martin, J. A. (2015). Dynamic managerial capabilities: Review and assessment of managerial impact on strategic change. *Journal of Management, 41*(5), 1281–1312.

Henkel, J. (2000). The risk-return fallacy. *Schmalenbach Business Review, 52*, 363–373.

Henkel, J. (2009). The risk-return paradox for strategic management: Disentangling true and spurious effects. *Strategic Management Journal, 30*, 287–303.

Herracleus, L., & Werres, K. (2016). On the road to disaster: Strategic misalignments and corporate failure. *Long Range Planning, 49*, 491–506.

Jegers, M. (1991). Prospect theory and the risk-return relation: Some Belgian evidence. *Academy of Management Journal, 34*(1), 215–225.

Johnson, H. J. (1992). The relationship between variability, distance from target, and firm size: A test of prospect theory in the commercial banking industry. *Journal of Socio-Economics, 21*(2), 153–171.

Kahneman, D., & Tversky, A. (1979). Prospect theory: An analysis of decision under risk. *Econometrica, 47*(2), 263–292.

Kunreuther, H., & Useem, M. (2018). *Mastering catastrophic risk: How companies are coping with disruption.* New York, NY: Oxford University Press.

Lustig, H., & Verdelhan, A. (2012). Business cycle variation in the risk-return trade-off. *Journal of Monetary Economics, 59*, 35–49.

Mandelbrot, B., & Taleb, N. N. (2006). A focus on the exceptions that prove the rule. *Financial Times*, March 23. Retrieved from http://www.ft.com/intl/cms/s/2/5372968a-ba82-11da-980d-0000779e2340.html#axzz2mDpbeON9

McKelvey, B., & Andriani, P. (2005). Why Gaussian statistics are mostly wrong for strategic organization. *Strategic Organization, 3*(2), 219–228.

McNamara, G., & Bromiley, P. (1997). Decision making in an organizational setting: Cognitive and organizational influences on risk assessment in commercial lending. *Academy of Management Journal, 40*, 1063–1088.

McNamara, G., & Bromiley, P. (1999). Risk and return in organizational decision making. *Academy of Management Journal, 42*, 330–339.

Miller, K. D., & Chen, W. (2003). Risk and firms' costs. *Strategic Organization, 1*, 355–382.

Nickel, M. N., & Rodriguez, M. C. (2002). A review of research on the negative accounting relationship between risk and return: Bowman's paradox. *Omega, 30*, 1–18.

Nicolis, G., & Prigogine, I. (1989). *Exploring complexity: An introduction.* New York, NY: Freeman

Nocco, B. W., & Stultz, R. M. (2006). Enterprise risk management: Theory and practice. *Journal of Applied Corporate Finance, 18*, 8–20.

Nordhaus, W. D. (2011). The economics of tail events with an application to climate change. *Review of Environmental Economics and Policy, 5*(2), 240–257.

Oviatt, B. M., & Bauerschmidt, A. D. (1991). Business risk and return: A test of simultaneous relationships. *Management Science, 37*, 1405–1423.

Prigogine, I. (1987). Exploring complexity. *European Journal of Operational Research, 30*, 97–103.

Ruefli, T. W. (1990). Mean–variance approaches to the risk–return relationship in strategy: Paradox lost. *Management Science, 36*, 368–380.

Ruefli, T. W. (1991). Reply to Bromiley's comment and further results: Paradox lost becomes dilemma found. *Management Science, 37*(9), 1210–1215.

Ruefli, T. W., Collins, J. M., & Lacugna. J. R. (1999). Risk measures in strategic management research: Auld lang syne? *Strategic Management Journal, 20*(2), 167–194.

Ruefli, T. W., & Wiggins, R. R. (1994). When mean square error becomes variance: A comment on "Business risk and return: A test of simultaneous relationships." *Management Science, 40*, 750–759.

Santacruz, L. (2019). Measures of firm risk-taking: Revisiting Bowman's paradox. *Managerial Finance, 46*(3), 421–434.

Scharfenaker, A., & dos Santos, P. L. (2015). The distribution and regulation of Tobin's q. *Economic Letters, 137*, 191–194.

Sharpe, W. F. (1964). Capital asset prices: A theory of market equilibrium under conditions of risk. *The Journal of Finance, 19*(3), 425–442.

Shefrin, H. (2007). Behavioral finance: Biases, mean–variance returns, and risk premiums. *CFA Institute Conference Proceedings Quarterly, 31*, 4–12.

Shefrin, H. (2014). Distinguishing rationality and bias in prices: Implications from judgments of risk and expected return. In T. J. Andersen (Ed.), *Contemporary challenges in risk management: Dealing with risk, uncertainty and the unknown* (pp. 7–49). London: Palgrave Macmillan.

Shefrin, H. (2016). How psychological pitfalls generated the global financial crisis. In T. J. Andersen (Ed.), *Routledge companion to strategic risk management* (pp. 269–295). Abingdon: Routledge.

Simkowitz, M. A., & Beedles, W. L. (1980). Asymmetric stable distributed security returns. *Journal of the American Statistical Association, 75*(370), 306–312.

Singh, J. (1986). Performance slack and risk taking in organizational decision making. *Academy of Management Journal, 29*, 562–585.

Singleton, J. C., & Wingender, J. (1986). Skewness persistence in common stock. *Journal of Financial and Quantitative Analysis, 21*(3), 335–341.

Sinha, T. (1994). Prospect theory and the risk return association: Another look. *Journal of Economic Behavior and Organization, 24*, 225–231.

Stulz, R. M. (1996). Rethinking risk management. *Journal of Applied Corporate Finance, 9*(3), 8–24.

Taleb, N. N. (2005). *Fooled by randomness: The hidden role of chance in life and the markets.* New York, NY: Random House. (First published in 2001.)

Taleb, N. N. (2007). *The black swan: The impact of the highly improbable.* New York, NY: Random House.

Taleb, N. N. (2013). *Antifragile: Things that gain from disorder.* London: Penguin Books.

Teece, D. J. (2007). Explicating dynamic capabilities: The nature and microfoundations of (sustainable) enterprise performance. *Strategic Management Journal, 28*, 1319–1350.

Teece, D. J., Pisano, G., & Shuen, A. (1997). Dynamic capabilities and strategic management. *Strategic Management Journal, 18*, 509–533.

Wang, H., Barney, J. B., & Reuer, J. J. (2003). Stimulating firm specific investment through risk management. *Long Range Planning, 36*, 49–59.

Williams, M. A., Baek, G., Park, L. Y., & Zhao, W. (2016). Global evidence on the distribution of economic profit rates. *Physica A, 458*, 356–363.

Wiseman, R. M., & Catanach, A. H. (1997). A longitudinal disaggregation of operational risk under changing regulations: Evidence from the savings and loan industry. *Academy of Management Journal, 40*(4), 799–830.

Wiseman, R. M., & Gomez-Mejia, L. R. (1998). A behavioral agency model of managerial risk taking. *Academy of Management Review, 23*(1), 133–153.

Chapter 6

Analyzing Manufacturing Subsamples

Abstract

In this chapter, we perform more detailed analyses and present the distribution characteristics and risk-return relationships of accounting-based financial returns (ROA) across different industry contexts and between periods with different economic conditions. We first display the frequency diagrams of the return measure (ROA) and its two components, net income and total assets, that show entirely different contours in the density graphs that must be reconciled. This is partially accomplished by analyzing the skewness, kurtosis, cross-sectional, and longitudinal risk-return characteristics of each of the three variables. The analyses further considers potential effects of accounting manipulation, and different organizational and executive traits, that identifies significant effects on the accounting-based return measures. We find extremely left-skewed return distributions with high negative correlations between the average return and risk measures, which reproduces the "Bowman paradox" as originally conceived. The same analysis is performed on net income and operating cash flows, the latter being less susceptible to accounting manipulation, which should display similar effects even though these performance distributions show positive skewness. We find negative but insignificant cross-sectional risk-return relations that nevertheless reappear in analyses performed within the specific industry contexts. The study further uncovers effects from prevailing economic conditions where left-skewness and kurtosis as well as negative risk-return correlations are much more significant during periods of high economic growth and business expansion where competition is more pronounced.

Keywords: Accounting manipulation; bankruptcy risk; executive overconfidence; financial crisis; maneuverability; strategic flexibility

A Study of Risky Business Outcomes: Adapting to Strategic Disruption, 83–97
Copyright © 2023 by Torben Juul Andersen
Published under exclusive licence by Emerald Publishing Limited
doi:10.1108/978-1-83797-074-220231006

Introduction

The preceding chapter outlined various theoretical perspectives adopted in empirical studies of firm performance and associated risk outcomes performed in the management and finance literatures and found some commonalities in findings across the different research streams. To ascertain these observations from empirical evidence further, we analyzed a comprehensive corporate dataset, the sampling of which is described earlier (see Chapter 2), and confined the analysis to the complete case of North American data on firm performance as is common practice in the empirical management literature. To simplify an otherwise too comprehensive task, we confined the ensuing analyses to consider (only) two accounting-based financial ratios and a market-based performance indicator. That is, we extracted annual data from the Standard & Poors Compustat North American database for the 25-year period 1995–2019[1] for all the firms operating in the manufacturing industries [SIC: 2000–3999] with a minimum of five years of consecutive data across the full period. Several earlier studies have focused on manufacturing companies, so this sampling provided a better basis for possible comparisons to earlier studies (e.g., Bromiley, 1991; Miller & Chen, 2003, 2004). This provides a total sample of 887 firms with complete case data throughout the period. Further inspection of the financial ratio (ROA), determined by net income as a percentage of total assets, identified two "extreme" outliers that seemed to clearly exceed the normal value range, that we examined in more detail to assess the reasons behind the extreme values. Both cases seemed to reveal extraordinary circumstances with major organizational reconstructions at play that argue for status as "true" outliers that will be excluded from the subsequent analyses.

We applied return on assets (ROA) as the key financial ratio in the ensuing analyses as a frequently adopted relative performance indicator with absolute profits compared to the total size of the firm. The corresponding risk indicators adopted was the standard deviation of ROA as calculated over each five-year period as is common practice in many prior studies (e.g., Andersen, Denrell, & Bettis, 2007; Fiegenbaum & Thomas, 1986, 1988, 2004). We used cash flow return (CFRE) determined as operating activities net cash flows (OANCF) as a percentage of total revenues, or sales to test results for robustness against an alternative performance measure. The corresponding risk measure was determined as the standard deviation of CFRE over five-year periods as before. To incorporate a market-based performance measure to compare results, we used Tobin's q (TQ) determined by the total market capitalization of the firm calculated as total shares outstanding multiplied by the official end-of-year stock price divided by the firm's book value of equity, or paid in capital and (accumulated) earnings retained. Since we are interested in performance and risk outcomes, we also

---

[1]The 1995–2019 time-period covers intervals depicting expansive growth, a dot.com bubble, global financial crisis, and steady economic recovery up until but not including the economic effects from the COVID-19 pandemic.

included Altman's Z^2 (ALT Z) as an alternative risk indicator reflecting the level of bankruptcy risk ascribed to the individual firm (Altman, 1983).

Analyzing the Data

As was uncovered from the analyses of imputed values from the original untreated European and North American datasets as well as the complete case samples collected from both geographical regions there are consistent left-skewed performance distributions with many (extreme) negative performers. To assess these findings further in the complete case data from North American firms operating in different manufacturing industries, we extracted the annual financial return (ROA) data for all firms in the sample and looked at the distribution of performance outcomes. As ROA is determined by two reported values, net income and total assets, it is interesting (and potentially very relevant) to hold the frequency distributions of ROA up against the comparable distributions of net income and total assets. To this effect, we plotted the annual data for net income, total assets, and ROA into their respective frequency diagrams for all firms throughout the 25-year period (Fig. 6.1). We observe distinctly different distribution patterns, which probably should not surprise even though these diagram plots are rarely taken into consideration in the empirical studies. The different contours of these interrelated distributions raise some obvious questions about their interactive relationships as they together determine the eventual relative performance indicator ROA.

We observe that net income follows a leptokurtic distribution with wide tails and a slight positive skewness not unlike the distribution observed on market-based returns. In contrasts, the distribution of total assets show power-law characteristics dominated by many small- to medium-sized companies and a (relatively) smaller number of very large firms. Observing these distributions does not immediately lead to an understanding or explanation of the eventual distribution formed by ROA that shows a left-skewed distribution of outcomes characterized by many (extreme) negative outliers. (Please note the comparison between annual and average annual data points (Fig. AI) in Appendix 6.1.) However, these relationships could be partially associated with the adoption of different accounting practices where managers have some possibilities to affect the timing and size of income and balance sheet items reported in the accounts. Adopting a common accounting practice of (linear) depreciation of long-term assets can impose large initial investment costs on the accounts that will underestimate the accounting-based returns of firms heavily invested in future development efforts, such as, younger start-up

---

[2]Altman's Z [ζ] (ALT Z) is determined by the equation $\zeta = 1.2A + 1.4B + 3.3C + 0.6D + 1.0E$, where

> A is the ratio of working capital divided by total assets,
> B is the ratio of retained earnings divided by total assets,
> C is the ratio of earnings before interest and tax divided by total assets,
> D is the ratio of the market value of equity divided by total liabilities, and
> E is the ratio of total sales divided by total assets.

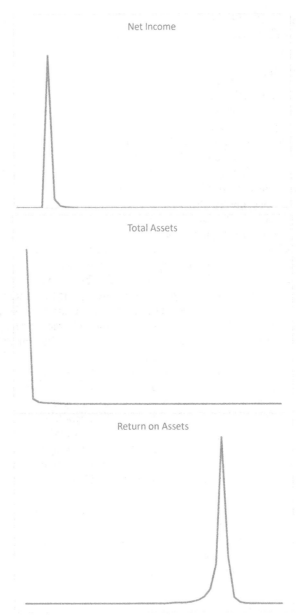

Fig. 6.1.   Frequency Diagrams of Net Income, Total Assets, and ROA (Annual Accounting Data 1995–2019).

companies. Conversely, these accounting practices can cause more mature and historically successful incumbents to overestimate their accounting performance. This uncovers likely effects of accounting practices and company size that should be considered when analyzing the accounting-based return data.

If we apply a different financial return measure like cash flow return (CFRE) as an alternative performance ratio, we find similar patterns where the net operating cash flows (OANCF) displays a slightly leptokurtic positively skewed distribution, whereas CFRE is negatively skewed. The performance measures of ROA and CFRE reflect accounting-based profits and cash inflows, respectively, but are quite highly correlated showing a correlation coefficient of 0.63 over the 25-year period. Interestingly, Tobin's q (TQ) that represents a market-based performance indicator has a negative co-variance with ROA with a correlation coefficient of -0.39 over the 25-year period. This suggests, that market-based returns derived from the development of stock prices, as they are affected by the future expectations of (all) investors in the market, may frequently develop in the opposite direction of the firm's realized accounting performance. That is, superior accounting-based performance measures may actually have a negative effect on, or an inverse relationship to, the markets' expectations about future performance. Conversely, disappointing market-based returns can underestimate the opportunities (good) management may generate to improve the firm's cash flows and realize higher future accounting-based performance.

Based on the data from the full sample of firms over the 25-year period, we present the descriptive statistics for the various performance (and risk) variables. The data for the accounting-based returns (ROA and CFRE) show (highly) negatively skewed performance measures with (very) high excess kurtosis. The skewness of ROA is around -3.3 and for CFRE it falls around -7.7, whereas the corresponding numbers for kurtosis amount to 15.8 and 71.0, respectively, which is far above the requirements for a normal distribution[3] (Table 6.1a).

Table 6.1a.   Descriptive Statistics on Key Performance Variables for Manufacturing Firms 1995–2019.[a]

	ROA	**CFRE**	**TQ**	**ALT Z**
Mean	0.11	0.02	1.79	1.37
Median	3.14	0.09	1.44	0.20
Kurtosis	15.80	74.01	24.46	1.14
Skewness	−3.28	−7.74	4.01	0.09

ROA, return on assets (net income divided by total assets); CFRE, cash flow return (cash flows from operations divided by total sales); TQ, Tobin's q (total market value of outstanding shares divided by the equity book value); ALT Z, Altman's Z (a five-factor indicator of bankruptcy risk).

[a] Calculated across all manufacturing firms in all years over the full period.

---

[3] The Kurtosis of a univariate normal, or Gaussian, distribution is 3, whereas distributions with Kurtosis above 3 are increasingly leptokurtic referred to as excess kurtosis. The Skewness of a symmetric normal distribution is 0, whereas distributions with Skewness below -1, or above $+1$, are said to be respectively negatively skewed, with a tail on the left side of the distribution, or positively skewed.

By comparison, we note that the market-based return indicator (TQ) has a positively skewed distribution with skewness of 4.0 and kurtosis around 24.5 indicating a highly leptokurtic distribution (Table 6.1a). This suggests that we can expect large variations in market-based performance across individual firms and between firms in different industry subsamples. The indicator of bankruptcy risk (ALT Z) is closer to the criteria for normally distributed outcomes with a skewness measure close to 0 and a kurtosis around 1, which is lower than the kurtosis observed in a normal distribution. This means that there are relatively few "outlying" observations and will display the contours of a so-called platykurtic frequency distribution.

Accounting and Leadership Effects

Various studies have found that managers tend to adjust reported earnings so they can avoid accounting-based losses while increasing the reported earnings, or profits. The phenomenon reflects (very) low frequencies of minor "decreases" in loss and earnings in the accounts compared to (very) high frequencies of minor "increases" in accounting-based income, or reported profits (Burgstahler & Dichev, 1997). This indicates a certain amount of conscious efforts among managers, or executive decision-makers to modify, adjust, or even manipulate the reported earnings to make firm performance look slightly better. Hence, when companies are operating at relatively low performance levels they may be more inclined to make the accounts look better than they currently are. It does indeed show in the data that when firms barely meet their earnings benchmark there are higher frequencies of performance adjustments as accruals are used opportunistically to manipulate the reported business activities while engaging in active earnings management (Di Meoa, Larab, & Surroca, 2017). To capture these incentives to manipulate the accounting-based performance measures, we adopt a control variable (BENCH), which is equal to 1, when net income (or the annual change in net income) divided by total assets falls between 0 and 0.01, or otherwise it takes the value of 0. This measure has been developed, used, and validated previously in other studies as a significant indicator of a mediocre performance range that captures the managerial incentive to manipulate the accounting-based performance (Gunny, 2010).

Another aspect of conscious managerial choices regards the extent to which the firm retains a certain flexibility in their ongoing investment commitments that otherwise might restrain the maneuverability in leadership decisions that could affect subsequent performance and risk outcomes. This kind of managerial flexibility influence can be captured by a measure that indicates the level of autonomy retained in the firm's investment decisions that provides wider room for maneuvering when the environmental conditions change over time. For this purpose, we determine the firm's level of autonomous investments (AUT), calculated as the cash flows generated from operations divided by total capital expenditures, as an indicator of the flexibility retained in the firm's ongoing investment decisions. Another possible indicator of flexibility is the firm's cash holdings (CASH), calculated as total cash and cash equivalent assets divided by total current liabilities, that captures the level of capital readily available for immediate, or relatively fast investments in business opportunities that can increase the capacity to respond to ongoing changes.

While the prior control variables constitute indicators of inherent flexibilities in the balance sheet and incentives for executives to manipulate the accounting-based return measures, we can also consider more "mental" aspects of the top managers, or the CEO of the company that may affect the way they make resource-committing decisions. Hence, we are aware of effects from (potential) executive biases linked to narcissistic, or hubristic traits of powerful leaders that may develop overly confident views on their own abilities over time that can have consequences for their decision-making competencies and outcomes (e.g., Owen & Davidson, 2009). That is, CEO overconfidence affects how s/he interprets performance feedback signals and thereby influences the risk-taking behavior in investment decisions (e.g., Schumacher, Keck, & Tang, 2020). Overconfident executives tend to have overly optimistic biases with a higher propensity to manipulate the reported accounting performance (Schrand & Zechman, 2012). These types of executives are typically subsumed within their own perceived reality of the surrounding environment that will guide their decisions seconded by their own previous experiences. Hence, overconfident executives typically have optimistic biases reflected in a certain willingness to take on more expansive and risky approaches including actively manipulating the company accounts.

The degree of CEO overconfidence has been measured by a firm specific score (Schrand & Zechman, 2012). This measure captures five excessive executive decision patterns compared to patterns observed in the general industry: level of investment, acquisition expenditure, debt-equity ratio, issuing esoteric debt instruments, and no dividend payouts.

1. Excess investment is captured by the regression coefficient of total asset growth on sales growth for the firm minus the similar coefficient calculated on aggregated industry data. A positive number indicates excess investment (score = 1, otherwise 0).
2. Excess acquisition expenditure compares firm M&A expenses as a ratio over total sales minus the average ratio for the industry. A positive difference suggests excess acquisition expenditures (score = 1, otherwise 0) reflecting a relatively aggressive M&A strategy with a strong belief in the future potential of the firm.
3. Excess debt load is reflected in the debt-equity ratio, measured as the firm's total outstanding debt as a ratio over total liabilities minus the equivalent average ratio for the industry. A positive difference suggests an abnormal propensity to assume external debt (score = 1, otherwise 0) and reflecting a willingness to further increase the gearing of retained earnings to expand the business.
4. Excess debt issuance is determined by whether or not the firm has issued more risky esoteric debt instruments, such as, convertible bonds or preferred stock (score = 1, otherwise 0).
5. Excess reinvestment of own funds is captured by the absence of dividend payments to the shareholders and indicated by whether the dividend payout ratio is zero or not (score = 1, otherwise 0), which corresponds to the firm's retention of all earnings for reinvestment in the future business development.

The overconfidence measure (OVER) takes on the value of 1, if the sum of the five individual scores exceeds, or is equal to 3, otherwise if the sum is below three, it takes on the value of 0, where each of the five indicators assume the value of 1, if confirmed, otherwise 0.

When analyzing the data for the four "managerial" variables, we observe that OVER, AUT, and CASH are positively skewed, whereas BENCH is negatively skewed (Table 6.1b). We further note that CASH and in particular AUT have (very) high excess kurtosis, which indicates a (very) leptokurtic distribution with a wide range of (extreme) outcomes and a potential for many outliers. Obviously, we should consider here that the annual data span over a wide variety of firms that operate in different industry contexts with their individual competitive dynamics as well as the adopted measures span across a 25-year period where business conditions and the management approaches adopted by the individual firms may vary over time.

To get a better sense of the data, we also analyzed the differences between firms with high and low performance in split samples above and below the median ROA of 3.14% (see Table 6.2a). The performance data of above and below performers are shown in Table 6.2a where we note positively skewed performance distributions of ROA, CFRE, and TQ (skewness of 2.2, 0.8, and 2.3) for the high performers compared to negatively skewed outcomes on ROA and CFRE (skewness of −3.0 and −5.7) for the low performers. The kurtosis for all performance measures in both the above and below subsamples is (very) high, and even excessively so, indicating leptokurtic distributions particularly in the below median subsample (11.3 and 38.2). The risk indicator (ALT Z) is substantially higher in the above median subsample (2.32 vs. 0.43) signifying that the high-performing firms (not surprisingly) have substantially lower default risk.[4]

Looking at the "managerial" measures across the above and below median subsamples (Table 6.2b) we note that CEO overconfidence (OVER) is lower among high performers compared to the low performers (0.15 vs. 0.21) possibly reflecting

Table 6.1b.   Statistics on Leadership and Accounting Variables for Manufacturing Firms 1995–2019.[a]

	OVER	AUT	CASH	BENCH
Mean	0.18	3.67	0.89	0.72
Median	0.00	2.05	0.32	0.78
Kurtosis	2.05	540.65	40.53	−0.05
Skewness	1.78	21.41	5.23	−0.85

OVER, Executive overconfidence (five indicators of overconfident executive behaviors); AUT, Autonomous investments (cash flows from operations divided by total capital expenditures); CASH, Cash holdings (total cash and equivalent assets divided by total current liabilities); BENCH, Bench (incentive to manipulate reported earnings in the accounts).

[a] Calculated across all manufacturing firms in all years over the full period.

---

[4] A high Altman's Z reflects a strong credit standing where a value above 3 is considered very strong while a value below 1.8 indicates a real, and increasing, potential for bankruptcy.

Table 6.2a.   Statistics for Firms Performing Above and Below Median ROA 1995–2019.[a]

	ROA	CFRE	TQ	ALT Z
Above				
Mean	7.11	0.14	1.83	2.32
Median	6.28	0.13	1.58	0.43
Kurtosis	8.57	1.47	8.79	0.63
Skewness	2.21	0.84	2.30	0.07
Below				
Mean	−6.93	−0.10	1.75	0.43
Median	−1.67	0.05	1.28	0.11
Kurtosis	11.26	38.19	21.21	0.90
Skewness	−3.03	−5.66	4.04	0.09

ROA, Return on assets (net income divided by total assets); CFRE, Cash flow return (cash flows from operations divided by total sales); TQ, Tobin's q (total market value of outstanding shares divided by the equity book value); ALT Z, Altman's Z (a five-factor indicator of bankruptcy risk).

[a] Calculated across all manufacturing firms in all years over the full period.

Table 6.2b.   Accounting and Leadership Statistics for Firms Above and Below Median ROA 1995–2019.[a]

	OVER	AUT	CASH	BENCH
Above				
Mean	0.15	8.06	0.80	0.91
Median	0.00	2.92	0.29	0.96
Kurtosis	3.51	305.03	48.75	3.35
Skewness	2.10	16.62	5.91	−1.66
Below				
Mean	0.21	−0.72	0.97	0.52
Median	0.00	1.03	0.34	0.56
Kurtosis	1.08	25.77	35.17	−0.23
Skewness	1.52	−2.06	4.73	−0.55
ANOVA[b]	0.00796	0.00049	0.12289	0.00000

OVER, Executive overconfidence (five indicators of overconfident executive behaviors); AUT, Autonomous investments (cash flows from operations divided by total capital expenditures); CASH, Cash holdings (total cash and equivalent assets divided by total current liabilities); BENCH, Bench (incentive to manipulate reported earnings in the accounts).

[a] Calculated across all manufacturing firms in all years over the full period.

[b] The p-value for difference between mean values.

an executive bias with a potential to inflict adverse performance effects. Flexibility in capital investment (AUT) is much higher among above median performers (8.0 against −0.7) whereas (interestingly) the opposite is the case with respect to CASH (0.8 against 0.97). To test the statistical significance of the observed differences, we used one-way ANOVA analysis that show highly significant differences between the mean-values of OVER, AUT, and BENCH but not on CASH, thus implying that low-performing firms in general hold as much cash as high-performing firms. The incentive to manipulate accounts (BENCH) is higher in the above median subsample (0.91 against 0.52) indicating that reported accounting-based income and performance measures are managed actively among high performers.

Industry-related Effects

The risk-return characteristics of ROA (a relative performance indicator of profits against total assets) and NI (net income; indicating the reported net profit) were analyzed across the full sample as well as across the different industry contexts (Tables 6.3a and 6.3b). The risk-return relationships can be determined as cross-sectional relationships over a given time period (typically five-year intervals) or as longitudinal relationships with different time-lags (of one, two, three, four, and five years) between the risk-taking actions and the subsequent performance outcomes. As observed in other studies (e.g., Andersen & Bettis, 2015), we find substantial negative cross-sectional risk-return correlations on the full sample (−0.67) whereas the longitudinal risk-return relationships gradually diminish as the time-lags increase (from −0.60 to −0.25). The industry specific subsamples in food processing (SIC: 2000–2092), apparel products (SIC: 2300–2390), steel works and metals (SIC: 3310–3390), vehicles and transportation equipment (SIC: 3700–3790, industrial instruments and equipment (SIC: 3800–3873) display similar relationships but with notable differences between industries.

The risk-return relationships have typically been analyzed based on relative accounting-based performance ratios like ROA (and ROE) following a tradition established by Bowman (1980) as he published his early seminal studies. However, it has been shown how a negatively skewed distribution of say ROA automatically will produce a negative risk-return relationship of significant size (e.g., Henkel, 2000, 2009; Ruefli, 1990), so the risk-return relationships based on ROA may overestimate the phenomenon. As the distribution of NI has a positive skew, this automatic relationship should not occur when we base the analysis on this performance measure. That is, the inverse risk-return effects should presumably be present in analyses based on NI and OANCF as performance measures, if the observed "Bowman paradox" is real. Therefore, we calculated the risk-return relations between NI and the coefficient of variation in NI as the appropriate corresponding risk indicator.[5] We observe that the full sample fails to show substantial negative risk-return relations on NI possibly due to the significant differences

---

[5]The coefficient of variation is determined as the standard deviation of NI divided by the average size of NI and is thereby neutralizing a potential size effect.

Table 6.3a. Risk-Return Correlations (ROA) of Manufacturing Firms 1995–2019.[a]

Risk-Return Correlations	Full Sample	Food 2000–2092	Apparel 2300–2390	Steel Works 3310–3390	Vehicles 3700–3790	Instruments 3800–3873
Cross-sectional	-0.67	-0.38	-0.45	-0.24	-0.57	-0.63
Longitudinal ($t-1$)	-0.60	-0.30	-0.48	-0.13	-0.45	-0.56
Longitudinal ($t-2$)	-0.51	-0.27	-0.53	0.00	-0.34	-0.49
Longitudinal ($t-3$)	-0.42	-0.25	-0.48	0.12	-0.25	-0.43
Longitudinal ($t-4$)	-0.33	-0.22	-0.42	0.27	-0.19	-0.37
Longitudinal ($t-5$)	-0.25	-0.20	-0.37	0.41	-0.17	-0.32

Return = Return on Assets (ROA); Risk = Standard Deviation in Return on Assets (SDROA).
[a] Calculated across all manufacturing firms in all years over the full period.

Table 6.3b. Risk-Return Correlations (NI) of Manufacturing Firms 1995–2019.[a]

Risk-Return Correlations	Full Sample	Food 2000–2092	Apparel 2300–2390	Steel works 3310–3390	Vehicles 3700–3790	Instruments 3800–3873
Cross-sectional	-0.04	-0.14	-0.27	-0.22	-0.17	-0.14
Longitudinal ($t-1$)	-0.04	-0.13	-0.27	-0.20	-0.16	-0.13
Longitudinal ($t-2$)	-0.04	-0.13	-0.27	-0.14	-0.15	-0.13
Longitudinal ($t-3$)	-0.04	-0.13	-0.21	-0.12	-0.13	-0.13
Longitudinal ($t-4$)	-0.04	-0.12	-0.17	-0.07	-0.12	-0.10
Longitudinal ($t-5$)	-0.04	-0.11	-0.13	0.00	-0.10	-0.09

Return = Net Income (NI); Risk = Coefficient of Variation in Net Income (CVNI).
[a] Calculated across all manufacturing firms in all years over the full period.

in the competitive dynamics across the different industry contexts (Table 6.3b). However, when we fine grain the analyses and calculate the risk-return relationships within each of the identified industries it uncovers substantial negative risk-return correlations although generally at lower levels that those observed from the analyses using ROA as the corresponding performance measure.

As we have observed how effects of common accounting practices, and possible manipulation of performance data particularly among large high-performance firms, it may provide somewhat misleading results. To circumvent that this is the case and as a further robustness check, we repeated the analyses based on cash flow return (CFRE) and net operating cash flows (OANCF) that are less susceptible to accounting manipulation and timing of income recording. This analysis uncovered largely comparable outcomes with substantially similar results. We also conducted the analyses based on winsorized data where extreme observations that fall outside of the mean value of ROA, plus and minus four standard deviations are eliminated from the data sample. However, that did not lead to materially different results. Hence, the negative risk-return relations do not (only) appear in samples of accounting-based performance measures like ROA, that are susceptible to income management and accounting manipulation, but they are also found when the analysis is performed on net income and operating cash flow data.

Effects of Economic Conditions

A number of prior studies have found possible effects from changing economic conditions as they evolve over time and appear in different time periods (e.g., Cool & Schendel, 1988; Cool, Dierickx, & Jamison, 1989; Fiegenbaum & Thomas, 1986). For this reason, we performed analyses of the performance data across different time-intervals over the 25-year period characterized by different economic conditions and business contexts. These analyses include three periods reflecting high-growth conditions over 1995–2005, followed by crisis and recession during 2006–2010, and finally economic recovery from 2011 to 2019 (Table 6.4a).

We observe negatively skewed performance distributions in each of three time-intervals but notice interesting differences as the negative skewness is substantially higher under the economic high-growth conditions (−5.36) compared to the recession (−0.89) and enduring recovery (−2.95). The excess kurtosis is similarly (extremely) pronounced in the period of the growth scenario (53.5) relative to the subsequent scenarios of financial crisis (15.5) and economic recovery (19.0). This seems to indicate, possibly (somewhat) at odds with common expectations, that competition and hence extreme negative (and positive) performance outcomes are more pronounced in the "good" times as opposed to in the "bad" times with economic crisis conditions. This and comparable effects may also be reflected in the associated risk-return relationships as they are determined across the same time-intervals (Table 6.4b).

Hence, we do observe substantially higher negative cross-sectional risk-return correlations during the high-growth period (−0.73) both compared to the period of financial crisis (−0.65) and the subsequent period of economic recovery (−0.61). This suggests that the leptokurtic features of accounting-based

Table 6.4a. Performance Outcomes of Manufacturing Firms by Subperiods.[a]

Time Period	1995–2005	2006–2010	2011–2019
Mean	1.28	1.63	3.06
Median	4.51	4.66	5.24
Kurtosis	53.52	15.54	19.03
Skewness	−5.36	−0.89	−2.95

Return on Assets (ROA).

[a] Calculated across all manufacturing firms in the years of the indicated periods.

Table 6.4b. Risk-Return Correlations of Manufacturing Firms by Subperiods.[a]

Time Period	1995–2005	2006–2010	2011–2019
Cross-sectional	−0.73	−0.65	−0.61
Longitudinal ($t - 1$)	−0.67	−0.64	−0.56
Longitudinal ($t - 2$)	−0.55	−0.60	−0.53
Longitudinal ($t - 3$)	−0.43	−0.42	−0.50
Longitudinal ($t - 4$)	−0.32	−0.28	−0.52
Longitudinal ($t - 5$)	−0.24	−0.25	−0.42

Return-Return = Correlation between return on assets and the standard deviation in return on assets.

[a] Calculated across all manufacturing firms in the years of the indicated periods.

performance measures reflected in high skewness and excess kurtosis, and the corresponding negative risk-return relationships, are associated with the competitive conditions in the industry, where competition is significantly more intense and pronounced under conditions of high economic growth.

Conclusion

The collected financial return data reproduce previous findings of left-skewed performance distributions with negative risk-return relationships that represent the so-called Bowman paradox. However, we find that the return measures are influenced by incentives to manipulate the accounts with outcomes affected by managerial traits of overconfidence and flexibility as well as periodically prevailing economic conditions.

References

Altman, E. (1983). *Corporate distress: A complete guide to predicting, avoiding and dealing with bankruptcy*. New York, NY: Wiley.

Andersen, T. J., & Bettis, R. A. (2015). Exploring longitudinal risk-return relationships. *Strategic Management Journal, 36*(8), 1135–1145.

Andersen, T. J., Denrell, J., & Bettis, R. A. (2007). Strategic responsiveness and Bowman's risk-return paradox. *Strategic Management Journal, 28*, 407–429.

Bowman, E. H. (1980). *A risk/return paradox for strategic management.* Working paper, WP 1107-80. Alfred P. Sloan School of Management, Massachusetts Institute of Technology, Cambridge, MA.

Bromiley, P. (1991). Testing a causal model of corporate risk taking and performance. *Academy of Management Journal, 34*(1), 37–59.

Burgstahler, D., & Dichev, I. (1997). Earnings management to avoid earnings decreases and losses. *Journal of Accounting and Economics, 24*, 99–126.

Cool, K., Dierickx, I., & Jamison, D. (1989). Business strategy, market structure and risk-return relationships: A structural approach. *Strategic Management Journal, 10*(6), 507–522.

Cool, K., & Schendel, D. (1988). Performance differences among strategic group members. *Strategic Management Journal, 9*(3), 207–223.

Di Meoa, F., Larab, J. M. G., & Surroca, J. A. (2017). Managerial entrenchment and earnings management. *Journal of Accounting and Public Policy, 36*, 399–414.

Fiegenbaum, A., & Thomas, H. (1986). Dynamic and risk measurement perspectives on Bowman's risk-return paradox for strategic management: An empirical study. *Strategic Management Journal, 7*, 395–407.

Fiegenbaum, A., & Thomas, H. (1988). Attitudes toward risk and the risk-return paradox: Prospect theory explanations. *Academy of Management Journal, 31*, 85–106.

Fiegenbaum, A., & Thomas, H. (2004). Strategic risk and competitive advantage: An integrative perspective. *European Management Review, 1*, 84–95.

Gunny, K. A. (2010). The relation between earnings management using real activities manipulation and future performance: Evidence from meeting earnings benchmarks. *Contemporary Accounting Research, 27*(3), 855–888.

Henkel, J. (2000). The risk-return fallacy. *Schmalenbach Business Review, 52*, 363–373.

Henkel, J. (2009). The risk-return paradox for strategic management: Disentangling true and spurious effects. *Strategic Management Journal, 30*, 287–303.

Miller, K. D., & Chen, W. (2003). Risk and firms' costs. *Strategic Organization, 1*, 355–382.

Miller, K. D., & Chen, W. (2004). Variable organizational risk preferences: Tests of the March–Shapira model. *Academy of Management Journal, 47*, 105–115.

Owen, D., & Davidson, J. (2009). Hubris syndrome: An acquired personality disorder? A study of US Presidents and UK Prime Ministers over the last 100 years. *Brain, 132*(5), 1396–1406.

Ruefli, T. W. (1990). Mean–variance approaches to the risk–return relationship in strategy: Paradox lost. *Management Science, 36*, 368–380.

Schrand, C. M., & Zechman, S. L. C. (2012). Executive overconfidence and slippery slope to financial misreporting. *Journal of Accounting and Economics, 53*, 311–329.

Schumacher, C., Keck, S., & Tang, W. (2020). Biased interpretation of performance feedback: The role of CEO overconfidence. *Strategic Management Journal, 41*(6), 1139–1165.

Appendix 6.1.

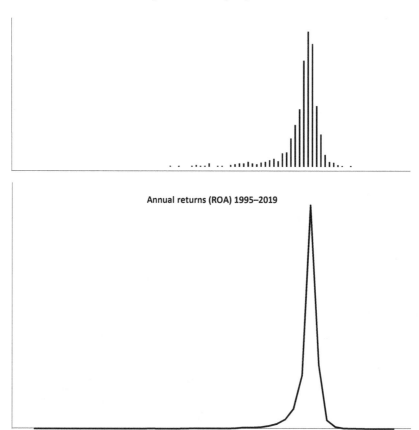

Average annual returns (ROA) 1995–2019

Annual returns (ROA) 1995–2019

Fig. AI.   Comparing Average Annual Data Points to Annual Data Points for the Full Period.

Note: The frequency distribution shown in the preceding analysis (shown in the bottom graph above) is based on ROA calculated for each individual firm in each of the 25 years over the period 1995–2019 reaching across a minimum return of −317.8% and a maximum return of 66.9%. We could also calculate the average return for each firms across all 25 years from 1995 to 2019 and then look at the distribution of average annual returns across the firms (top graph in the figure above). In this case, the range of values is reduced to minimum return of −79.5% and a maximum return of 32.7%.

Chapter 7

Simulating Strategic Adaptation

Abstract

This chapter explores other theoretical explanations to the commonly observed phenomenon of negatively skewed performance outcomes and inverse risk-return relationships in empirical firm data. The analysis conducted in many prior studies have implicated direct causal dependencies between performance and risk, or vice versa, with the possibility of simultaneous two-way relationships that are harder to discern. It is also shown how spurious artifacts deriving from the arithmetic links between mean and variance associate left-skewed distributions with negative mean variance correlations. However, the heterogeneous display of response capabilities among firms that compete in the same industry contexts may provide an alternative explanation for the observed performance characteristics. This is expressed as strategic responsiveness where performance outcomes with high negative skewness and excess kurtosis derive from heterogeneous adaptive processes among firms as they respond to a dynamic environment with different degrees of success. We test these results in different simulated competitive contexts disrupted by major unexpected events and find robust results across different environmental scenarios. The analysis looks at two different response processes, one modeled as conventional adaptive planning following an annual budget cycle, and another modeled as interactive updating where executives have frequent informative budget discussions with operating managers in the firm. The computational simulations show that interactive updating generates outcomes with higher returns and lower performance risk for moderate learning levels and restructuring costs. However, the resulting performance distributions are not as left-skewed as those observed in the empirical data that show higher resemblance to the adaptive planning outcomes.

Keywords: Computational modeling; disruptive events; interactive strategy-making; managing risk events; organizational learning; planned adaptation; strategic fit

A Study of Risky Business Outcomes: Adapting to Strategic Disruption, 99–119

Copyright © 2023 by Torben Juul Andersen

Published under exclusive licence by Emerald Publishing Limited

doi:10.1108/978-1-83797-074-220231007

Introduction

The prior analyses of comprehensive data on corporate performance show highly leptokurtic negatively skewed distributions of financial returns among firms both across European and North American markets (e.g., Albæk & Andersen, 2021). This might reflect that some firms are better equipped to respond, adapt, and persevere under turbulent economic conditions where abrupt events disrupt business processes (often) with extreme outcomes that challenge prevailing strategies, whereas (many) firms are affected adversely and fall into a fat tail of negative performers. In the following, we analyze these effects by applying a strategic responsiveness model that can generate computational simulation outcomes for comparison with the empirical evidence on the commonly observed negative skewed returns and inverse risk-return relationship. The results from this analysis suggest that heterogeneous strategic response capabilities across competing firms can explain these common artifacts. We discuss the implications of this insight for research and management practice.

General Background

The management field has typically used prospect theory (Kahneman & Tversky, 1979) and behavioral theory of the firm (Cyert & March, 1963) as underlying rationales for studies of the relationship between return and risk (and *vice versa*). That is, the way individual decision-makers perceive the current conditions and their prospects affect the decisions they make. Hence, situations framed by poor firm performance is assumed to induce risky decision behaviors while conditions of superior firm performance supposedly leads decision-makers to become more risk averse. The behavioral arguments derive at comparable outcomes as firm performance above an aspiration level determined by prior performance outcomes can lead to risk-averse behaviors, whereas performance below prior levels can drive risk-seeking behaviors. These implied psychological, or behavioral effects are (often) used to explain the "Bowman paradox" where firms across industries are generally found to have negative relationships between average returns and variance (or standard deviation) in returns as an indicator of risk (Bowman, 1980). As discussed previously (see Chapters 5 and 6) numerous subsequent studies have reproduced the inverse risk-return relations (e.g., Bromiley, 1991; Fiegenbaum & Thomas, 1988; Santacruz, 2019; Singh, 1986). It has also been demonstrated that negative risk-return relationships derive from spurious effects linked to the left-skewed return distributions due to the arithmetic relationship between average performance and associated risk measures (e.g., Henkel, 2000, 2009; Ruefli, 1990, 1991).

However, from a strategic adaptation perspective the left-skewed performance outcomes and inverse risk-return relations can (possibly) derive from diverse adaptive capacities generated by strategic response capabilities that enable some firms to respond faster and more effectively to unexpected changes (Bettis & Hitt, 1995). This idea is related to the concept of dynamic capabilities defined as an "ability to integrate, build, and reconfigure internal and external competences to address rapidly changing environments" (Teece, Pisano, & Shuen, 1997, p. 516).

Dynamic capabilities have been conceptualized around three fundamental organizational processes of sensing environmental changes, seizing responsive opportunities, and then restructuring organizational activities to accommodate the emergent events and environmental changes (Teece, 2007). A comparable organizational process is referred to as strategic responsiveness where the environmental changes are observed by managers operating within competing firms that engage in more or less effective responses to deal with the disruptive events with the aim of achieving a good fit with current market needs that is commensurate with higher performance outcomes (Andersen, Denrell, & Bettis, 2007). That is, effective ongoing responses to emergent disruptive events and developments should lead a firm to realize higher average returns with lower variation in performance outcomes over time. Hence, it is argued that successful strategic adaptation in rapidly changing environments may cause some firms to realize higher returns at lower performance risk, if the strategic leaders can impose decision structures, information processing, and organizational behaviors that are conducive to generate effective strategic responsiveness (Andersen, 2021).

Strategic Responsiveness

Strategic outcomes and hence the (realized) strategy is (theoretical) shaped by the actions that organizations take in resource committing decisions with the purpose of achieving intended aims where good strategic decisions lead to better performance reflected in higher and more stable trajectories of financial returns. This perspective is commensurate with Bowman's (1980) initial inclination that execution of "good management" skills can lead to both higher performance outcomes and lower variance in these outcomes. It assumes that the strategic management process can support an ability to generate effective responsive moves to accommodate ongoing changes in the environment thereby (effectively) adapting the business activities, that define the strategy, so they better match the requirements in the business context at all and any given points in time. We can express a generic strategic responsiveness model in a performance function that determines the effects of ongoing adaptation to rapid changes in the environment. As various firms display different abilities to respond to rapid unexpected and potentially extreme changes, the model reflects the fact that competing firms operating within a given industry context display heterogeneous strategic response capabilities. Some firms are more effective at adapting their strategic business activities to the changing context whereas quite a few other firms are not so effective adaptors. The model assumes that firm performance (partially) is a function of the fit between the strategic position of the firm and the market conditions at given points in time as argued in strategic reference point theory (e.g., Fiegenbaum, Hart, & Schendel, 1996). That is, if the business activities of a given strategic position provide a good match in response to the prevailing requirements of the competitive context, it is assumed to lead to higher firm performance because customer needs are (better) satisfied with (better) adoption of effective operational processing technologies. Therefore, the firms that are able to identify and determine the ongoing changes in the environment, and adjust their business activities accordingly to match the current requirements, will generate higher revenues, as they satisfy market demands and thus sell more, while also operate more efficiently at lower cost with lower inventory levels and (better) use of available technologies. This is a logic that resonates with a resource-based view where superior firm performance outcomes can derive from the consistent application of unique firm specific response capabilities (Barney, 1986, 1991, 2002; Winter, 1995).

When environmental conditions are changing rapidly, and possibly abruptly so, the ability to maintain a good fit between business activities and prevailing market demands hinges on a capacity to sense the ongoing changes and develop effective responses that provide a better strategic fit between the firm's strategic position and the current competitive conditions. In this context, some firms are better at assessing the utility and efficacy of alternative resource combinations and thus acquire the necessary resources at lower costs compared to their competitors (e.g., Barney, 1986). This logic underpins the economic effect of strategic response capabilities that can identify available resources and activate them in effective responses to observed, or anticipated environmental changes (e.g., Andersen et al., 2007; Teece et al., 1997).

A Computational Model

We can formalize the strategic responsiveness dynamic in a quantitative performance model where firms able to respond perfectly to the changing environmental conditions and thereby match and satisfy the requirements in the current market conditions will generate optimal performance outcomes. Conversely, firms that are unable to match current market conditions will suffer a penalty that corresponds to the gap between the firm positions and the requirements in the market. The optimal performance level is denoted K where imperfectly adapted firms will realize a performance outcome somewhat below the optimal level, K. The performance function for period t looks as follows:

$$R_t = K - b|c_t - d_t|a - C_t \qquad (1)$$

R_t = performance, or return, for a firm in time-period t.
K = maximum possible firm performance in the industry.
c_t = the prevailing business conditions at time-period t.
d_t = actual position held by the firm in time-period t.
$|c_t - d_t|$ = mismatch between business conditions and firm position at time t.
a, b = exponential and linear coefficients that affect the mismatch penalty.
C_t = adjustment costs associated with adaptive responses in period t.
t = consecutive time-periods, for example, years or quarters [$t = 1, 2, 3, ..., T$].

In this model specification, c_t denotes a strategic parameter at time t, for example, total demand, product feature, operating practice, process technology, or the like, whereas d_t denotes the firm's position on that parameter at time t after having responded to observed changes in the previous period $t - 1$. People in the firm (managers and employees) observe the changes as they happen and engage in adaptive responses to accommodate these changes and thereby match the environmental conditions in the subsequent period. For every period as time proceeds, the firms will try to reposition their activities so they provide a better match with the business conditions at all times: $t = 1, 2, 3, ..., T$. From this, we can see intuitively how firms that have effective response capabilities, so they are able to match the changing business conditions, will generate high returns (R_t) with relatively little variation in returns over time unless the adjustment costs (C_t) associated with the responses are excessive.

The coefficients b and a are always positive $(b > 0, a > 0)$, so any deviations from the perfect fit $(|c_t - d_t| > 0)$ will generate a mismatch penalty where the resulting suboptimal performance is influenced by the linear (b) and exponential (a) coefficients where larger coefficients cause higher mismatch penalties as reflective of more competitive, or hostile industry contexts.

We might consider that the optimal performance level in the industry (K) could vary and develop in a stochastic manner rather than assuming a constant fixed value, whereby the potential returns vary with changes in the economic conditions and changes over time would be expressed as:

$$K_t = K_0 + \sum_{p=1}^{t} K_p; \text{ where } K_p = N(K_0, \sigma)$$

The simple model with one strategic parameter could in principle also be extended to consider and incorporate a larger number (M) of parameters $(d_{1,t}, d_{2,t}, d_{3,t}, ..., d_{m,t}, ..., d_{M,T})$, which would expand the performance function as follows:

$$R_t = K - \Sigma b|c_{m,t} - d_{m,t}|^a - C_t; t = 1, 2, 3, ..., T; m = 1, 2, 3, ..., M$$

While these extensions in some way could present a more realistic setting, they do not (really) change the implied effects of the model but rather introduce a more complicated and in effect impose unnecessary computational intricacies. Hence, we chose to adopt the simple one-parameter performance model to ease the interpretation of the ensuing analytical outputs.

Firms are only rarely able to completely match the prevailing market conditions from period to period for various reasons including cognitive limitations, rigid structures, inertial behaviors, high uncertainty, etc., thus making it difficult to predict developments accurately. To reflect these flaws and embedded uncertainties, we could model c_t and d_t to develop in a stochastic manner in accordance with a normal distribution with variance σ^2 and mean μ evolving as a stationary stochastic process. But, business conditions are arguably formed by consecutive events influenced by human interventions linked over time in path-dependent ways. So, the evolving business context (c_t) is more accurately described as a path-dependent random process. A stochastic process even if stationary (3) makes it hard to predict conditions exactly, but they rarely move far distances beyond the mean $(\mu = c_0)$. By comparison, a business context that follows a path-dependent random walk (4) can actually wander quite a distance away from the mean value for extended periods of time.

Stationary stochastic process:

$$c_t = c_0 + \sum_{p=1}^{t} c_p; \text{ where } c_p = N(c_0, \sigma) \tag{3}$$

Path-dependent random walk:

$$c_t = c_0 + \sum_{p=1}^{t} c_p; \text{ where } c_p = N(c_{p-1},\sigma) \qquad (4)$$

Firm activities are influenced by individual managers (and employees) whose collective responses can be conceived as an adaptive learning process performed through the engagement of intelligent and observant individuals who due to cognitive limitations operate under conditions of bounded rationality. That is, firm responses can be captured as a stationary stochastic process (5) where outcomes are random to some extent. However, given the active engagement of individuals, the firm responses appear more realistically described as an adaptive learning process (6) where organizational agents and decision-makers develop new insights from different degrees of learning (l).

Static stochastic process:

$$d_t = d_0 + \sum_{p=1}^{t} d_p; \text{ where } d_p = N(d_0,\sigma) \qquad (5)$$

Adaptive learning process:

$$d_t = (l)c_{t-1} + (1-l)d_{t-1}; \, l = \text{ learning rate, } 0 < l < 1 \qquad (6)$$

Hence a better and more realistic specification of strategic responsiveness as enacted in a firm involves an adaptive learning process that responds to a business environment that evolves in accordance with a path-dependent random walk. This model specification will generate performance distributions with cross-sectional and longitudinal risk-return relationships that to a large extent are compatible with those observed in the empirical data (Andersen & Bettis, 2015).

Different Adaptive Processes

The computational strategic responsiveness model describes strategic adaptation that evolves as changes are observed and responsive actions are devised to adjust business activities so they provide a better fit with the prevailing environmental conditions (e.g., Andersen, 2021, 2023). This adaptive process can be depicted as central planning monitored through diagnostic strategic controls where the realized outcomes are compared to the existing plans on a regular basis often in line with an annual budget cycle. Observed mismatches between market developments and firm's position then informs the need for strategic responses that can update the current plans and develop an adjusted action plan for execution over the coming period (Fig. 7.1).

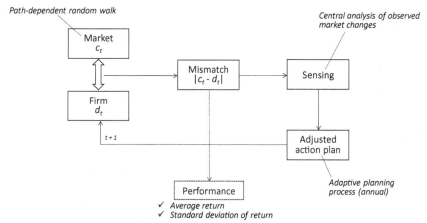

Fig. 7.1.   A Central Planning Model of Strategic Adaptation.

However, it has been noted that adaptive responses based on input from different engaged stakeholders can lead to more effective outcomes after disruptive changes and extreme events have occurred (e.g., Van der Vegt et al., 2015). That is, effective strategic adaptation can thrive on updated information generated by the experiences operating managers acquire as they take responsive initiatives to ongoing changes in their respective task environments (e.g., Bower & Gilbert, 2005; Burgelman, 1996; Burgelman & Grove, 2007). Gaining more frequent access to these current insights from dispersed managers who operate in different parts of the organization can inform the central planning considerations and foster an adaptive dynamic in support of updated adjustments to the strategic action plans (e.g., Andersen, 2015a, 2015b; Andersen & Hallin, 2016). This more frequent updating of current insights, say quarterly as opposed to annually, can be achieved through an interactive control process that engages the local operating managers in open interactive discussions with top management as they review budgets and adjust the action plans on an ongoing basis to better understand the business conditions as the environment changes and generate better responses (Fig. 7.2).

Interactive controls is a way for top management to gain a better understanding of the changing environmental context based on discussions of "annual profit plans or budgets, second year forecasts, and strategic operating and financial plans" (Simons, 1995, p. 109) as a useful basis to update strategic action plans. The interactive discussions between senior executives at the corporate center and local operating managers can benefit from insights about current market changes observed in the operating entities to update action plans more frequently, say every quarter as opposed to annually (e.g., Andersen & Torp, 2019). Interactive updating that collects insights from dispersed operating entities can provide more frequent assessments of ongoing environmental changes compared to adaptive planning and simple linear projections (Fig. 7.3).

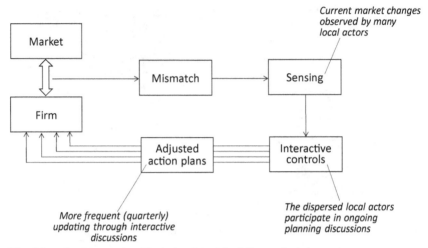

Fig. 7.2.   An Interactive Updating Model of Strategic Adaptation.

Simple linear predictions in volatile markets require that the projected path follows an accurate trend line into the future but even if the linear prediction is fairly accurate, it will fail to capture and accommodate all the minor market changes that may arise along the way (Fig. 7.3, linear projection). Adaptive responses generated through central planning constitutes a more long-cycled retrospective process tied to the annual cadence of the budgeting and strategic planning systems with a better approach to update strategic action plans (Fig. 7.3, central planning). However, updating action plans through interactive discussions between top management and dispersed managers can gain more frequent access to current insights as an even better approach for more frequent adaptive moves that align the firm more closely to evolving changes in the business environment (Fig. 7.3, interactive control). From this we assert that interactive updating provides more effective strategic response capabilities in the sense that it can create a better fit with the environmental conditions at various points in time.

In the strategic responsiveness model this should generate higher and more stable performance developments because the mismatch penalties are comparatively smaller. However, these positive adaptation effects from interactive information exchanges hinge on some basic assumptions, for example, that executives are receptive to insights from lower-level managers and that the firm has a flexible organizational structure to enable adaptive responses. In short, we must consider the potential influence of adjustment costs associated with imbedded learning processes and ensuing reorganization efforts to reconfigure the business activities so they fit the evolving environmental context. If the adjustment costs are excessive, the adaptive moves might not be viable, or economical at least not as more frequent endeavors. Hence, the following analyzes these trade-offs under different business conditions comparing planned adaption with interactive updating.

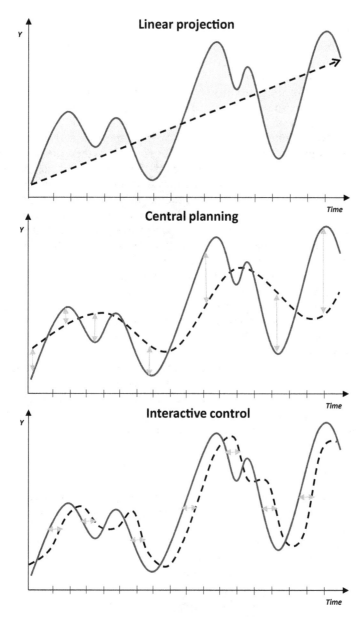

Full line = ongoing development in the business environment (c_t)
Dotted line = updated perception of the business environment (c_t)
Grey areas and arrows = indicators of (potential) mismatch ($c_t - c_t$)

Fig. 7.3. Different Approaches to Strategic Adaptation.

Computational Analyses

The model provides a platform that can generate periodic performance out-comes from simulations across firms operating in specified industry contexts. The return data generated by the computational model will allow us to examine the characteristics of the performance distributions, and the cross-sectional and longitudinal risk-return relationships. These simulations determine average per-formance and performance variations by firm for predetermined time-intervals here set at 40 consecutive time-periods (to be interpreted as quarters or years). The cross-sectional risk-return relationship is calculated as the correlation coeffi-cient between average returns and the standard deviation in returns on simulated performance outcomes over five-year periods generated from samples of 5,000 firms in each industry context. The longitudinal risk-return relations are calcu-lated as the correlations between the standard deviation in returns over five-year periods and the average returns over subsequent five-year periods in line with prior studies (e.g., Fiegenbaum & Thomas, 1986, 1988; Miller & Bromiley, 1990).

We intend to investigate the performance effects of adaptive planning com-pared to interactive updating considering different levels of organizational fric-tion expressed by the associated adjustment cost. We conduct the performance analysis for different learning rates ranging between 0 and 1 in intervals of one decimal point to capture effects of embedded learning processes construed as adaptive planning and interactive updating. The associated adjustment costs con-stitute expenses incurred to assess environmental information and execute organi-zational restructuring efforts that adapt the business activities from one period to the next. The costs are determined by the relative magnitude of the changes made in the firm position ($|d_t - d_{t-1}|$). The related cost function (7) assumes that adjust-ment expenses are incurred from a certain cost basis (ρ) that reflects the amount of resources required to complete the adaptive efforts.

$$C_t = f[\rho * |d_t - d_{t-1}|] \tag{7}$$

The initial firm position (d_0) is set at 100 in the simulation model and updated period by period as the business context changes as determined by the learning rate (l). The maximum possible performance level (K) is set at 100 in all the simu-lations with profitability penalized by an amount commensurate with the abso-lute difference, or mismatch, between the market and firm position ($|c_t - d_t|$) and the adjustment costs (C_t). The simulations were run with a linear coefficient of one ($b = 1$) and an exponential coefficient of two ($a = 2$). We incorporated three levels of adjustment cost, none ($\rho = 0$), low ($\rho = 10$), and high ($\rho = 25$), to assess the effects of organizational friction.

The simulation results indicate that in the absence of any adjustment costs it pays off to learn and adapt to the fullest extent because no resources are required to engage in the learning deliberations and there is no friction at all when exe-cuting the adaptive moves. Under these conditions, interactive updating is supe-rior to adaptive planning at all levels of learning and will lead to higher average performance with lower performance risk at the same time (Fig. 7.4). Hence, the strategic adaptation processes improve the level of performance with higher average returns and low standard deviation in returns. The corresponding effects on the inverse cross-sectional and longitudinal risk-return relations are shown in Appendix 7.1. Here we observe that the cross-sectional risk-return correlation is negative and high and only slightly decreasing in size for higher learning rates while the negative longitudinal risk-return relationship is considerably lower and moves toward zero as the learning rate increases to 1.

As the adjustment costs increase from low to high, learning and perfect adaptation is no longer favorable but show an optimal performance effect at a learning rate of 0.5–0.6 in the case of adaptive planning and a learning rate around 0.2–0.3 in the case of interactive updating (Fig. 7.4). If the adjustment costs are high, strategic adaptation in the form of interactive updating underperforms adaptive planning at higher learning rates ($l > 0.5$). In short, when environmental sensing and restructuring is more resource demanding and hence (increasingly) costly, the organizational learning efforts have diminishing return effects with optimal performance occurring at lower learning rates in environments described and specified as a path-dependent random walk.

Effects of Major Disruptions

To analyze the effects of different environments with major disruptive events, we specify two scenarios of abrupt environmental changes and large one-time losses. Sudden changes in the competitive context with potentially dramatic outcomes, for example, caused by industry shifts or other external events, such as, a pandemic (say COVID-19), or military conflict (say war in Ukraine). We incorporate these incidents in the model first by imposing periodic shifts in business conditions ($c_6 = +10$, $c_{15} = -10$; $c_{23} = +10$, $c_{31} = -10$) over the 40 time-periods ($T = 40$). Secondly, we incorporate major value write downs in two consecutive periods with negative profit effects ($P_{15}, ..., P_{18} = -100/4$; $P_{27}, ..., P_{30} = -100/4$) over the 40 simulation periods. We retain a low adjustment cost environment ($\rho = 10$) in these computations. The simulations show that interactive updating continues to outperform as a more effective strategic adaptation approach with optimal learning rates around 0.4–0.7 (Fig. 7.5). In the case of abrupt business changes, interactive updating remains more effective at all learning rates whereas one-time loss events reduces the advantage at higher learning rates ($l > 0.5$).

We further consider the effects of specific industry contexts expressed as more volatile business conditions and higher competitive hostility among industry peers. The first environmental condition is incorporated by increasing the standard deviation of the path-dependent random walk from two to three in the simulations [$d_p = N(d_0, \sigma)$; $\sigma = 3$]. The second condition of higher competitive hostility is incorporated by augmenting the penalty from environmental mismatch increasing the exponential parameter in the profit function from two to three [$K - b|c_t - d_t|^a$; $a = 3$]. The computational simulations show that interactive updating remains more effective than adaptive planning at all learning

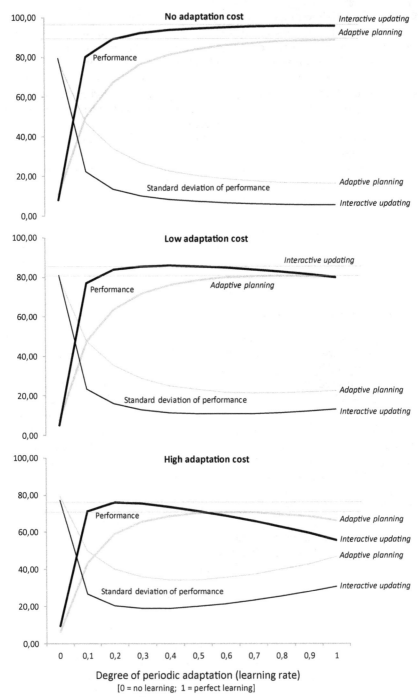

Fig. 7.4.   The Effects of Adaptation Cost on Strategic Adaptation.

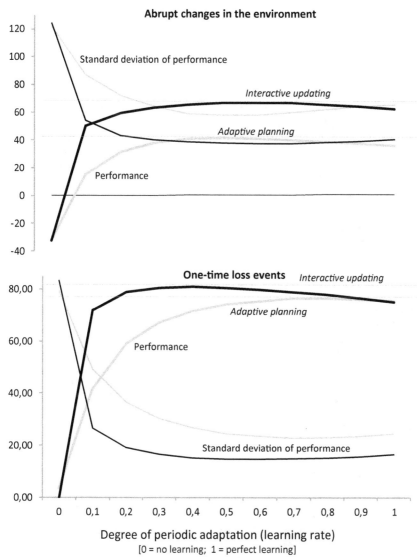

Fig. 7.5. The Effects of Environmental Jolts on Strategic Adaptation.

rates in both high volatility and more competitive business environments (Fig. 7.6).

To analyze the effect on performance of the two adaptation modes in the strategic responsiveness model, we plotted the frequency distributions of performance outcomes from interactive updating and adaptive planning in two comparative base scenarios (Fig. 7.7). From this we observe that the responsiveness model produces left-skewed performance outcomes with adaptive planning being more

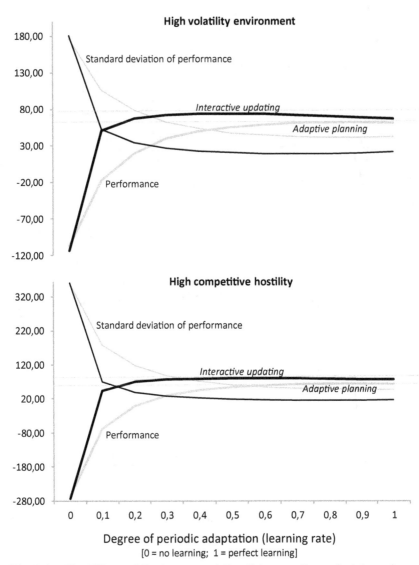

Fig. 7.6.   The Effects of Environmental Conditions on Strategic Adaptation.

left-skewed than interactive updating. In the base-scenario the cross-sectional risk-return correlation is −0.85 under interactive updating and −0.91 under adaptive planning thus confirming that the model reproduces the inverse risk-return relationships associated with negative skewness in the performance distribution (e.g., Henkel, 2009). In the strategic responsiveness model, this is a function of

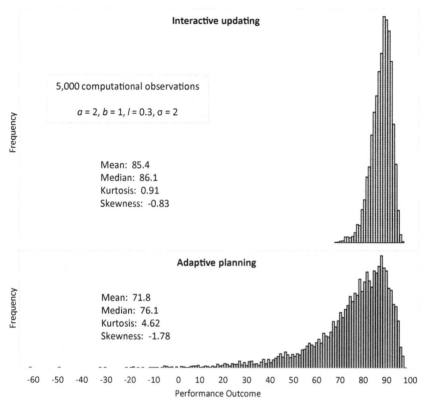

Fig. 7.7. The Frequency Distributions of Simulated Performance Outcomes.

environmental uncertainty and competitive hostility where higher values of σ (the stochastic variability) and the exponential parameter a (the mismatch penalty) are associated with more left-skewed performance outcomes and larger absolute negative risk-return relationships.

It is observed how the effects of adaptive planning and interactive updating are significantly different and constitute possible sources for heterogeneous strategic response capabilities among firms that typically operate in accordance with their own distinct management approaches. We further note how cognitive limitations, inertia, structural rigidity, and other types of organizational friction expressed in associated adjustment costs influence the relative effectiveness of different strategic adaptation processes in specified business contexts.

Hence, the preceding simulation results from the computational strategic responsiveness model demonstrates that different configurations of the strategic adaptation process can reproduce the commonly observed features of the left-skewed performance distributions and negative risk-return relationships.

Empirical Validation

Adaptive planning depicts a strategic updating mode linked to the top management team as central conveners of strategic thinking and periodic revisions to the strategic actions plans. This process is more exposed to characteristic features of the executives that may display cognitive biases and inertial behaviors to different degrees that eventually can influence the flexibility of the firm and the associated adjustment costs. Interactive updating describes a more inclusive strategic updating mode where the top managers listen to current insights from operating managers with a willingness to learn from it around more frequent budget discussions thereby implying faster adjustments to action plans. By comparison then, a centralized planning approach should be more exposed to influences of executive overconfidence (e.g., Schrand & Zechman, 2012) and be more susceptible to flexible structures compared to interactive updating. We cannot discern from our empirical dataset the underlying strategic updating processes applied by the various sampled firms, so comparisons across updating approaches will depend on more detailed data gathering and thus remain speculative assessments although arguably based on sound theoretical reasoning. What we can test based on the available data, however, is what the apparent effects over executive overconfidence and flexibility from autonomous investments are on performance, distribution, and risk-return outcomes. To assess these potential effects, we used the measures of CEO overconfidence (OVER) and autonomous investments (AUT) developed in Chapter 6 to assess their relationships to the characteristics of the performance distributions. We perform this assessment through simple comparisons between firms ranged above and below the mean levels on the OVER and AUT measures (Table 7.1).

Table 7.1.   The Performance and Risk-Return Outcomes in Different Subsamples 1995–2019.[a]

Periods	Overconfidence (<Mean)	Overconfidence (>Mean)	Autonomous (>Mean)	Autonomous (<Mean)
Minimum	−99.0	−98.6	−24.9	−99.0
Maximum	32.7	24.8	32.7	13.1
Mean	0.68	−0.48	5.15	−4.88
Median	3.52	2.72	5.47	0.31
Standard dev.	12.8	12.6	5.8	15.4
Kurtosis	17.9	14.0	4.5	9.8
Skewness	−3.5	−3.1	−0.5	−2.8
Cross sectional	−0.68	−0.75	−0.53	−0.72

[a] Calculated as average value for all firms within the subsample in all years over the period.

We observe that firms with more overconfident executives realize lower mean returns (−0.48%) compared to firms with non-overconfident executives (0.68) with higher absolute negative risk-return relationships ascribed to less flexible firms (AUT below the mean). A flexible organizational structure with relatively low friction will enable the reconfiguration of resources and business processes at lower adjustment costs and therefore display more effective response capabilities. The degree of flexibility is also reflected in the level of autonomous investments the firms can engage in. When we compare the performance of firms with high and low levels of autonomous investments (in Table 4), it is noted how autonomous firms score higher mean returns (5.15%) compared to non-autonomous firms (−4.88%) with a lower absolute negative risk-return relationship (−0.53). These observations are consistent with the results obtained from the strategic responsiveness model and expected outcomes from organizations characterized by lower friction and flexible adaptive strategic updating.

Discussion and Conclusion

The computational strategic responsiveness model generates performance outcomes from various simulations to explore important antecedents of effective response capabilities. As organizations are confronted with abrupt and disruptive business contexts they face unexpected events with potentially extreme outcome effects. In these settings, effects of imperfect information, cognitive biases, and inertia in rigid organizational structures with high adjustment costs inhibit the ability to respond effectively. This demonstrates how dynamic resource orchestration in effective adaptive responses is associated with distinct performance advantages (Barney, 1986).

Strategic adaptation is modeled as imperfect learning (low learning rate) responding to a random path-dependent business environment where effective adaptation is associated with higher performance and lower performance risk reflected in inverse risk-return relationships. Even at low adjustment costs it is no longer viable to engage in unlimited learning and optimal updating is reached at learning rates around 0.2–0.4. The strategic responsiveness model reproduces the left-skewed performance distributions and inverse risk-return phenomena observed in empirical performance data. In turbulent business contexts with adjustment costs, a low learning rate generates the highest performance and lowest performance variance. Environments exposed to environmental shocks caused by changing competitive paradigms or various crisis scenarios can generate performance and risk trajectories comparable to those observed in the empirical performance data.

The computational analyses demonstrate that effective strategic response capabilities are associated with superior performance by simultaneously generating higher returns and lower standard deviations in returns. The computational analysis assumes that a good strategic fit with current competitive conditions is rewarded with higher returns whereas a mismatch is penalized as the firm fails to deliver what customers want and adopt inefficiently outdated technologies. So, competitive industry contexts with heterogeneous response capabilities among firms have few high performers and many underperformers reflected in left-skewed performance distributions and inverse risk-return relations.

The computational model results demonstrate how different approaches to strategic updating, such as, adaptive planning and interactive updating, can provide a basis for heterogeneous response capabilities. Hence, we derive from this that firms with openness to absorb updated insights from the operating entities of the firm while maintaining a flexible structure can generate low-cost responses to rapid environmental changes and generate superior more stable performance outcomes.

The computational and empirical analyses show the potential superiority of interactive updating as a better representation of effective strategic response capabilities in rapidly changing environments. However, the empirical data do not reflect circumstances where a majority of firms assume these superior approaches to strategic adaptation.

References

Albæk, M., & Andersen, T. J. (2021). The distribution of performance data: Consistent evidence of (extreme) negative outcomes. In T. J. Andersen (Ed.), *Strategic responsiveness for a sustainable future: New research international management* (pp.147–174). Bingley: Emerald Group Publishing.

Andersen, T. J. (2015a). Strategic adaptation. In J. D. Wright (Ed.), *International encyclopedia of the social & behavioral sciences* (Vol. 12, pp. 501–507). Amsterdam: Elsevier.

Andersen, T. J. (2015b). Interactive strategy-making: Combining central reasoning with ongoing learning from decentralised responses. *Journal of General Management*, *40*(4), 69–88.

Andersen, T. J. (2021). Dynamic adaptive strategy-making processes for enhanced strategic responsiveness. In T. J. Andersen (Ed.), *Strategic responsiveness for a sustainable future: New research international management* (pp. 49–65). Bingley: Emerald Publishing.

Andersen, T. J. (2023). Adaptive strategy-making and left-skewed performance outcomes. In T. J. Andersen (Ed.), *Responding to uncertain conditions: New research on strategic adaptation* (pp. 17–39). Bingley: Emerald Publishing.

Andersen, T. J., & Bettis, R. A. (2015). Exploring longitudinal risk-return relationships. *Strategic Management Journal*, *36*(8), 1135–1145.

Andersen, T. J., Denrell, J., & Bettis, R. A. (2007). Strategic responsiveness and Bowman's risk-return paradox. *Strategic Management Journal*, *28*, 407–429.

Andersen, T. J., & Hallin, C. A. (2016). The adaptive organization and fast-slow systems. In R. J. Aldag (Ed.), *Oxford research encyclopedias: Business and management* (pp. 1–26). New York, NY: Oxford University Press. https://doi.org/10.1093/acrefore/9780190224851.013.126

Andersen, T. J., & Torp, S. (2019). Achieving adaptive responsiveness through strategic planning, autonomous strategic actions, and interactive controls. In T. J. Andersen, S. Torp, & S. Linder (Eds.), *Strategic responsiveness and adaptive organizations:*

Simulating Strategic Adaptation 117

New research frontiers in international strategic management (pp. 61–80). Bingley: Emerald Publishing.

Barney, J. B. (1986). Strategic factor markets: Expectations, luck, and business strategy. *Management Science, 32*(19), 1231–1241.

Barney, J. B. (1991). Firm resources and sustained competitive advantage. *Journal of Management, 17,* 99–120.

Barney, J. B. (2002). *Gaining and sustaining competitive advantage.* Upper Saddle River, NJ: Prentice Hall.

Bettis, R. A., & Hitt, M. A. (1995). The new competitive landscape. *Strategic Management Journal, 16,* 7–19.

Bower, J. L., & Gilbert, C. G. (Eds.). (2005). *From resource allocation to strategy.* New York, NY: Oxford University Press.

Bowman, E. H. (1980). A risk–return paradox for strategic management. *Sloan Management Review, 21*(3), 17–31.

Bromiley, P. (1991). Testing a causal model of corporate risk taking and performance. *Academy of Management Journal, 34*(1), 37–59.

Burgelman, R. A. (1996). A process model of strategic business exit: Implications for an evolutionary perspective on strategy. *Strategic Management Journal, 17*(S1), 193–214.

Burgelman, R. A., & Grove, A. S. (2007). Let chaos reign, then rein in chaos—Repeatedly: Managing strategic dynamics for corporate longevity. *Strategic Management Journal, 28*(10), 965–979.

Cyert, R. M., & March, J. G. (1963). *A behavioral theory of the firm.* Hoboken, NJ: Prentice Hall.

Fiegenbaum, A., Hart, S., & Schendel, D. (1996). Strategic reference point theory. *Strategic Management Journal, 17*(2), 219–235.

Fiegenbaum, A., & Thomas, H. (1986). Dynamic and risk measurement perspectives on Bowman's risk-return paradox for strategic management: An empirical study. *Strategic Management Journal, 7,* 395–407.

Fiegenbaum, A., & Thomas, H. (1988). Attitudes toward risk and the risk-return paradox: Prospect theory explanations. *Academy of Management Journal, 31,* 85–106.

Henkel, J. (2000). The risk-return fallacy. *Schmalenbach Business Review, 52,* 363–373.

Henkel, J. (2009). The risk-return paradox for strategic management: Disentangling true and spurious effects. *Strategic Management Journal, 30,* 287–303.

Kahneman, D., & Tversky, A. (1979). Prospect theory: An analysis of decision under risk. *Econometrica, 47*(2), 263–292.

Miller, K. D., & Bromiley, P. (1990). Strategic risk and corporate performance: An analysis of alternative risk measures. *Academy of Management Journal, 33,* 756–779.

Ruefli, T. W. (1990). Mean–variance approaches to the risk–return relationship in strategy: Paradox lost. *Management Science, 36,* 368–380.

Ruefli, T. W. (1991). Reply to Bromiley's comment and further results: Paradox lost becomes dilemma found. *Management Science, 37*(9), 1210–1215.

Santacruz, L. (2019). Measures of firm risk-taking: Revisiting Bowman's paradox. *Managerial Finance, 46*(3), 421–434.

Schrand, C. M., & Zechman, S. L. C. (2012). Executive overconfidence and slippery slope to financial misreporting. *Journal of Accounting and Economics, 53,* 311–329.

Simons, R. (1995). *Levers of control: How managers use innovative control systems to drive strategic renewal.* Boston, MA: Harvard Business School Press.

Singh, J. (1986). Performance slack and risk taking in organizational decision making. *Academy of Management Journal, 29,* 562–585.

Teece, D. J. (2007). Explicating dynamic capabilities: The nature and microfoundations of (sustainable) enterprise performance. *Strategic Management Journal, 28,* 1319–1350.

Teece, D. J., Pisano, G., & Shuen, A. (1997). Dynamic capabilities and strategic management. *Strategic Management Journal, 18*, 509–533.

Van der Vegt, G. S., Essens, P., Wahlström, M., & George, G. (2015). Managing risk and resilience, *Academy of Management Journal, 58*(4), 971–980.

Winter, S. G. (1995). Four Rs of profitability: Rents, resources, routines, and replication. In C. A. Montgomery (Ed.), *Resource-based and evolutionary theories of the firm: Towards a synthesis* (pp. 147–178). New York, NY: Springer.

Appendix 7.1

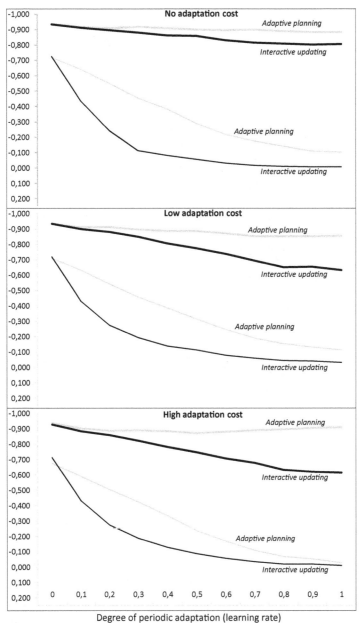

Fig. AI. Cross-Sectional and Longitudinal Risk-Return Relations. Degree of periodic adaptation (learning rate):[0 = no learning; 1 = perfect learning].

Chapter 8

Examining the Outliers

Abstract

In this chapter, we first examine the distribution characteristics of firm performance across different competitive industry contexts and periodic economic conditions of growth, recession, and recovery. There is mounting evidence that the contours of accounting-based economic returns consistently display (extreme) left-skewed leptokurtic distributions with negative risk-return relationships, which implies the existence of many negative performance outliers and some positive outliers. We note how negative skewness, excess kurtosis, and inverse risk-return relationships prevail in industries with more intense competition and in economic growth scenarios where more innovative initiatives compete. As the study of outliers typically is ignored in mainstream management studies, we extract a total of 23 extreme performers using a conventional winsorization technique that identifies 16 negative and 7 positive outliers. We study the performance trajectories of these firms over the full period and find that negative performers typically operate in capital-intensive innovative industries whereas positive performers operate in activities that cater to prevailing demand conditions and expand the business in a balanced manner. The firms that under- and over-perform as measured by the financial return ratio both constitute smaller firms compared to the total sample and show how relative movements in the ratio numerator and denominator affect the recorded return measure. However, the negative outliers generally use their public listing to access capital for investment in more risky development efforts that require a certain scale to succeed and thereby limits their flexibility. The positive outliers appear to expand their business activities in incremental responses to evolving market demands as a way to enhance maneuverability and secure competitive advantage by honing their unique firm-specific capabilities.

Keywords: Left-skewed returns; extreme outcomes; leptokurtic distribution; maneuverability; negative outliers; positive outliers; response capabilities

A Study of Risky Business Outcomes: Adapting to Strategic Disruption, 121–142
Copyright © 2023 by Torben Juul Andersen
Published under exclusive licence by Emerald Publishing Limited
doi:10.1108/978-1-83797-074-220231008

Introduction

Contemporary firms operate in dynamic market contexts and those organizations that are able to adapt to these changing and disruptive conditions are expected to persevere and generate superior long-term performance outcomes. The competitive environment appears to be increasingly erratic where emergent risk events, such as, pandemic, cyberattack, military conflict, or geopolitical tension may take firms by surprise with things often evolving in unpredictable ways. These conditions can impose major losses on firms as a possible cause for left-skewed economic outcomes. We seem to observe a trend toward more stochastic development paths with potentially extreme outcomes that fail to comply with the assumptions of the normal distribution. It reflects a competitive landscape with rapid competitive moves, radical technological innovations, and abrupt political changes where disruptive events generate increasingly uncertain conditions where it is impossible to meaningfully predict or foresee what is coming.

Under uncertain conditions humans may cling to conventional interpretations and models as the means to feel in control although it may represent a false sense of security. Hence, we tend to underestimate the prevalence of random events and largely ignore the possibility of rare extreme developments (e.g., Taleb, 2005, 2007, 2013). We continue to apply linear statistical methodologies to uncover basic relationships in management science even though the analyses based on Gaussian statistics often are wrong. As a consequence, we typically also dismiss closer examination of outliers, that is, firms with extreme performance outcomes, that otherwise could be important sources for more detailed insights to explain both positive and negative performance trajectories (McKelvey & Andriani, 2005). A close examination of outliers may provide a better understanding of (the) complex interdependencies that can trigger events toward extreme outcomes but we normally ignore such opportunities to generate new knowledge (Baum & McKelvey, 2006; Boisot & McKelvey, 2011).

Despite the unpredictable nature of emergent risk events that affect the competitive environment, firms must be able to respond to them and adapt their business activities to accommodate uncertainty with potentially radical occurrences that are not adequately described by standard analytical approaches (Nordhaus, 2011). Hence it observed that poorly performing firms also appear to be those most vulnerable and exposed to economic shocks as a major reason for left-skewed outcomes and negative risk-return relations (Becerra & Markarian, 2021). Prior studies including the analyses of comprehensive performance data for European and North American firms, presented in the previous chapters, find regular patterns of (extreme) left-skewed financial returns and negative risk-return relationships on accounting-based economic indicators (Albæk & Andersen, 2021).

Financial Return Analysis

The previous chapters examined distribution characteristics of financial returns including skewness, kurtosis, and risk-return relations based on the complete case sample of manufacturing firms operating in different industrial sectors (see Chapter 6). In addition to the full sample, we identified three industry sub-sets that often are assumed to represent different degrees of dynamic change and competitive pressures. The first subset is comprised by firms in "consumer goods" including food, apparel, and other manufactured products that we typically con-sider as constituting basic necessities where the demand is less sensitive to changes in economic conditions. The second subset of "competitive" firms were identified in industries that often are seen as entailing more intense competition including industries like pharmaceuticals, machinery, equipment, air and spacecraft, mineral products, and scientific instruments (e.g., European Commission, 2007). The third "knowledge-based" subset included firms operating in innovative sectors like biop-harma, diagnostics, publishing, industrial machinery, semiconductors, and analyti-cal instruments. Hence, we analyze the performance outcomes of the full dataset and across the consumer goods, competitive, and knowledge-based industry subsets. Looking at the numbers, we observe substantial negative skewness and very high excess kurtosis both in the full sample as well as the industry subsamples (Table 8.1).

It is noted how knowledge-based firms in innovative industries realize lower mean returns with a higher standard deviation in outcomes compared to firms in consumer goods. The average ROA in knowledge-based industries amounts to −0.20% for the full 25-year period from 1995 to 2019 compared to 1.27% in consumer goods and 1.56% in the competitive industries. The standard deviation in financial returns (ROA) over the period is lowest in consumer goods (13.5) compared to the knowledge-based (18.5) and competitive (19.3) industries. The kurtosis and skewness measures are less pronounced among firms in the knowledge-based industries (7.6 and −2.0) compared to firms in consumer goods (13.9 and −2.7) and particularly those operating in competitive industries (19.8 and −3.2). We speculate this may reflect that knowledge-based assets are more flexible and

Table 8.1. Financial Returns (ROA) of Firms in Manufacturing Industries 1995–2019.[a]

Industries	Full Sample	Consumer Goods	Competitive	Knowledge-based
Minimum	−79.5	−76.1	−123.4	−90.8
Maximum	32.7	28.9	41.0	39.2
Mean	0.33	1.27	1.56	−0.20
Median	3.16	4.03	5.35	4.32
Standard dev.	11.8	13.5	19.3	18.5
Kurtosis	11.2	13.9	19.8	7.6
Skewness	−2.8	−2.7	−3.2	−2.0
N	883	228	207	232
Cross-sectional R/R	−0.67	−0.70	−0.67	−0.64

[a] Calculated as average returns for all firms in the subindustries during the entire period.

easier to reconfigure and therefore will be associated with less friction and lower adjustment costs. So, higher flexibility to restructure is supposed to facilitate adaptation at lower costs, which is associated with lower negative skew and less extreme outcomes in the performance distribution. We might expect this to also be reflected in a somewhat lower absolute negative cross-sectional risk-return correlation in the knowledge-based industries (−0.64), which is what we seem to observe from the data.

We often assume that firms operating in the consumer goods industries are less sensitive to different exogenous events due to more steady demands for products that are required to maintain our daily lives. In contrast, we might expect firms in competitive industries to be comparatively more sensitive to abrupt environmental changes, whereas firms in knowledge-based industry sectors might be more flexible and adaptive when they face major disruptions. Hence, we do observe higher negative skewness and excess kurtosis in the competitive versus the consumer goods and knowledge-based industries and find more left-skewed distributions associated with more negative cross-sectional risk-return correlations. This might suggest that "Bowman's paradox" is partly a function of the competitive nature of the industry and the firms' ability to adapt to ongoing changes. In short, different industry contexts represent different degrees of extreme negative outcome tails where the outliers are likely to represent different dynamic conditions, adaptive processes, and economic effects.

Various earlier studies have observed different performance effects as the economic conditions change over consecutive time periods (e.g., Cool, Dierickx, & Jamison, 1989; Cool & Schendel, 1988; Fiegenbaum & Thomas, 1986). To test and reproduce earlier findings, we can analyze the financial return (ROA) data over time intervals that are clearly associated with different business cycle conditions, such as high economic growth from 1995 to 2005, crisis and recession from 2006 to 2010, and subsequent economic recovery from 2011 to 2019 (Table 8.2).

Table 8.2.   Return Outcomes and Risk Correlations of Manufacturing Firms by Subperiods.[a]

Time-period	1995–2005	2006–2010	2011–2019
Return on Assets (ROA)			
Average	1.28	1.63	3.06
Median	4.51	4.66	5.24
Standard dev.	18.12	15.12	13.39
Maximum	49.08	41.96	42.40
Minimum	−216.64	−113.23	−100.10
Kurtosis	53.52	15.54	19.03
Skewness	−5.36	−0.89	−2.95
Cross-sectional R/R	−0.73	−0.65	−0.61

Looking across these periods of time, we observe substantially higher negative skewness in returns and cross-sectional risk-return relations during the turbulent high-growth period (−5.36 and −0.73) compared to the financial crisis (−0.89 and −0.65) and the ensuing period of economic recovery (−2.95 and −0.61).

In short, the empirical data collected in an extensive North American sample of manufacturing firms confirm the prevalence of fat negative tails in the performance distributions where a substantial number of firms consequently must be performing rather poorly whereas the tails of positive performers is comparatively much smaller. We want to analyze the firms located in the negative and positive tails of the performance distribution in more detail with the intent to form a better understanding the dynamic associated with these consistently observed phenomena.

Identifying the Outliers

The complete case data sample described and analyzed in previous chapters (see Chapters 6) excludes two extreme outliers identified by simple examination of the financial return values (ROA). To account for outliers the "usual way," we subsequently winsorized the data around four standard deviations from the mean return (ROA). This singed out another 21 firms in the sample as outliers thus making a total of 23 firms that represent relatively extreme performance outcomes, or outliers. These firms were identified based on their average performance outcomes generated over the 25-year period 1995–2019 and thus represent results from across the different subperiods (Table 8.2) and different types of industrial sectors (Table 8.1). Due to the historical contents of these performance outcomes, we had to examine these firms in more detail by applying "forensic" techniques, which implies collecting and examining publicly available information sources to uncover prior corporate information and assess the firm-specific conditions that caused the observed performance developments including various business activities and important strategic actions. For each of the 16 negative outliers (average returns below the mean value of all firms minus four times the standard deviation) and 7 positive outliers (average returns above the mean value of all firms plus four times the standard deviation), we listed a description of the firm with its key characteristics (Table 8.3). The forensic approach can obviously not claim to represent an exact science. Nonetheless, the systematic process of gathering public information across comparable subsamples of firms provides a broad foundation of data that can validate the formative characteristics that emerge around these firms and the industrial contexts they operate in.

Consistent with the prior data analyses of below-median performers, we note that the negative outliers typically operate in the development of medical equipment or related products (7 of 16 firms), in technology-intense industries (5 of 16 firms), and in research-driven activities (2 of 16 firms). That is, the vast majority of firms among the negative outliers consist of organizations engaged in research and development activities related to medical equipment, or other advanced technologies, that constitute rather risky and capital-intensive venture activities. It is symptomatic that seven of the firms were eventually acquired and consolidated

Table 8.3.   Description of Negative and Positive Outliers from Sampled Manufacturing Firms 1995–2019.

Company (gvkey)	Descriptive Characteristics[a]
16 Negative Outliers (ROA outcomes below the mean minus four times the standard deviation)	
SQI Diagnostics Inc. (162934)	R&D intense going concern developing proprietary technologies and products with modest asset base and high negative income – delisted 2019 (https://sqidiagnostics.com/)
Sunrise Technology Intl. Inc. (15470)	Producer of dental equipment and supplies – filed for Chapter 7 bankruptcy in 2002 – assets acquired by PriaVision, Inc. in 2007 (https://www.prweb.com/releases/2007/04/prweb522600.htm)
Chromadex Corp. (177367)	Going concern in dietary supplements and food ingredients with both assets and negative net income growing more or less in parallel (https://investors.chromadex.com/overview/default.aspx)
Advanced Tissue Sciences Inc. (14836)	Innovative firms developing bio-engineered replacement skin for burn victims – went bankrupt in 2002 with losses growing faster than assets (https://www.latimes.com/archives/la-xpm-2002-oct-12-fi-tissue12-story.html)
United Energy Corp. (31024)	A going concern as a diversified oil and gas producer with significant increases in acquired energy assets – company delisted in 2010 (https://www.unrgcorp.com/)
Amerityre Corp. (63798)	Engaged in R&D and production of polyurethane foam tires – variable increases in assets with consistent but slightly decreasing losses – delisted in 2019 (https://amerityre.com/flat-free-tires/mower-tire-size-15x600-6/)
Soligen Technologies Inc. (28157)	Going concern engaged in web-based CAD-driven cast metal part production services – steady assets with slightly decreasing losses – delisted in 2000 (https://www.soligen.com/)
Disc Inc. (26247)	Service provider of media digitization established in 1982 – shows increasing assets and mounting losses – company delisted in 2002 (https://www.sec.gov/Archives/edgar/data/891788/000089161803003368/f91172e8vk.htm)
Ancor Communications Inc. (30131)	Manufacturing of computer communications equipment – increasing assets and volatile negative earnings – delisted in 1999 and acquitted by QLogic (https://money.cnn.com/2000/05/08/deals/qlogic/)

C-Phone Corp. (30625)	Production of telephone and telegraphic equipment – a somewhat steady level of assets and persistent loss development – delisted in 2000 (https://www.sec.gov/rules/final/34-52029.pdf)
Ariel Corp. (31455)	A going concern manufacturing separable reciprocating gas compressors – delisted in 2001 and run as a private company (https://www.arielcorp.com/compressors/compressor-landing-page.html)
Diasys Corp. (31300)	Development and manufacturing of diagnostic system solutions – assets slightly decreasing with steady losses – a going concern delisted in 2008 (https://www.diasys-us.com/)
Bioject Medical Technologies (14395)	Devices for liquid medication through the skin – volatile assets and persistent losses – delisted in 2010 and partially acquired by Inovio Pharma in 2016 (https://www.crunchbase.com/acquisition/inovio-pharmaceuticals-acquires-bioject-medical-technologies--9e588cec)
Vidamed Inc. (60906)	Treatment of urological disorders – volatile assets and persistent losses – delisted and acquired by Medtronic in 2002 (https://www.nytimes.com/2001/12/07/business/company-news-medtronic-to-buy-vidamed-for-326-million.html)
Cardiodynamics Intl. Corp. (2299)	Producer of electro-medical/electrotherapeutic equipment – assets increasing with erratic profit/loss development – acquired by SonoSite, Inc. in 2009 (https://www.sonosite.com/blog/sonosite-completes-acquisition-cardiodynamics-cardiovascular-disease-management-company)
Innovative Gaming Corp. (28333)	Innovative gaming technologies – assets decreasing with persistent losses – went bankrupt in 2001 with assets sold to Xertain, Inc. (https://lasvegassun.com/news/2000/feb/07/innovative-gaming-sells-assets/)

7 Positive Outliers (ROA outcomes above the mean plus four times the standard deviation)

Graco Inc. (5252)	Design and manufacturing of fluid handling products and solutions sold globally – a going concern with steadily increasing assets and profits (https://www.graco.com/us/en/homeowner/product/17g177-magnum-prox17.html)
Armanino Foods (21506)	Producer of upscale frozen and refrigerated Italian-style food – stable earnings development and balanced asset growth (https://armaninofoods.com/)

(Continued)

Table 8.3.   (*Continued*)

United-Guardian Inc. (10902)	Development and production of proprietary pharmaceutical and healthcare products – steadily increasing earnings and assets (https://u-g.com/)
Lotus Pharmaceuticals Inc. (163088)	Large Taiwanese pharmaceutical company with US activities – dramatic increases in assets and profits – delisted in 2010 (https://www.lotuspharm.com/company)
WD-40 Company (11234)	Manufacturer of household multi-use branded products – steadily growing assets and profits with slightly declining but high return levels (https://wd40.dk/)
Vitreous Glass Inc. (108769)	Trademarked waste treatment and disposal business removing contaminates from glass recycling glass sand for insulation – steady increase in assets and earnings (https://www.vitreousglass.ca/)
Waterfurnace Renewable (28030)	Production of geothermal heat pumps and energy products – increasing profits and assets at high returns – acquired by NIBE in 2014 (https://www.nibe.com/investors/pm-news-acquisitions-other/2014-news-acquisitions-other/2014-08-22-nibe-completes-acquisition-of-waterfurnace)

[a] See Appendix 8.1 for more detailed analysis of the companies.

into (successful) companies in the industry, whereas four firms were delisted thereby (formally) gaining more freedom to restructure business activities going forward, whereas in fact (only) two of these firms went into bankruptcy. So, the extreme negative tail of performers in the complete case dataset of manufacturing firms to a large extent represent research- and development-driven business activities that may see a public listing of their stock as the means to access external capital that can support their (ambitious) growth aspirations. As described, these firms may actually constitute an important segment for innovative business development efforts in technology-intense and knowledge-based industry sectors. These organizations have limited flexibility in their deployment of invested capital while operating practices and ongoing decisions are geared to satisfy success criteria of research and technological breakthrough and business expansion that can reward the committed resources in capital-intensive investments.

By comparison, the positive outliers represent quite diverse business activities and are comprised by firms that operate within pharmaceuticals, food processing, branded household goods, technology-based manufactured products or provide environmental solutions offering unique products and services. The diverse companies seem to adjust their business activities in a steady incremental manner as the economic conditions evolve. They appear to prosper by responding steadily to a growing market need emboldening demand by pushing distinctive product features and creating competitive advantage from idiosyncratic capabilities and competence-based offerings. These organizations seemingly execute a continuous string of small adaptive responses engaging flexible response capabilities guided by a business philosophy and value proposition that help materialize the strategic aims.

Discussion

The analyses outlined in the preceding chapters present empirical insights on the distribution of firm performance and risk-return outcomes across different time periods and industry contexts that consistently show (extreme) negative skewness and excess kurtosis of accounting-based returns with inverse risk-return features. These results are consistent with earlier studies that uncover heavy-tailed leptokurtic performance distributions (e.g., Williams, Baek, Park, & Zhao, 2016). We then extracted both negative and positive outliers from the sampled manufacturing firms where the former exceed the latter in number as a reflection of the left-skewed performance distribution.

We do not discern a specific size effect from this sample of outliers. The average size of total assets across the entire dataset for all firms over the full period amounts to USD 2,685 million, whereas the average for the negative outliers is USD 8.4 million and for the positive outliers USD 45.9 million. So, both the negative and positive outliers are considerably smaller in size compared to the full sample and the average size of the positive outliers is somewhat higher than the average size of the negative outliers. However, if we exclude the largest of the positive outliers, the average asset size amounts to USD 18 million, whereas the average size of the four largest negative outliers is USD 21.5 million. In other words, it is hard to claim that the extreme negative outlier phenomenon primarily relates to small-sized companies. Yet, it is observed in prior studies that nonnormal left-skewed returns are represented by firms with somewhat shorter life spans (e.g., Dichev, Graham, Harvey, & Rajgopal, 2013), which is consistent with the evidence observed in this outlier analysis.

Looking at the detailed data analysis conducted on each of the underperforming firms, we notice that high negative return ratios (ROA) typically are associated with increasing losses, or a negative net income development, where total assets generally grow at a slower pace than the losses (see Appendix 8.1). This contravenes some of the arguments for effects of linear depreciation practices where substantial asset investments in the initial development periods make the denominator of the return ratio (ROA) higher and thereby reduces the return measure. This only applies to situations of positive net income developments and not to situations of persistent losses as observed among the negative outliers. Conversely, the positive outliers appear to display steadily increasing profits where the business is expanded in a way that the increase in total assets follow the pace of the increasing earnings and thereby do not dilute the return ratio. In other words, the high performers show an ability to manage their business expansion in a balanced manner whereby profits and invested capital more or less follow in tune over time. Hence, we can argue that this constitutes a strategic response capability whereby the capital investment flexibility is retained as the business expands and grows.

References

Albæk, M., & Andersen, T. J. (2021). The distribution of performance data: Consistent evidence of (extreme) negative outcomes. In T. J. Andersen (Ed.), *Strategic responsiveness for a sustainable future: New research international management* (pp. 147–174). Bingley: Emerald Publishing.

Baum, J. A., & McKelvey, B. (2006). Analysis of extremes in management studies. In D. J. Ketchen & D. D. Bergh (Eds.), *Research methodology in strategy and management* (Vol. 3, pp. 123–196). Bingley: Emerald Publishing.

Becerra, M., & Markarian, G. (2021). Why are firms with lower performance more volatile and unpredictable? A vulnerability explanation of the Bowman paradox. *Organization Science, 32*(5), 1327–1345.

Boisot, M., & McKelvey, B. (2011). Connectivity, extremes, and adaptation: A power-law perspective of organizational effectiveness. *Journal of Management Inquiry, 20*(2), 119–133.

Cool, K., & Schendel, D. (1988). Performance differences among strategic group members. *Strategic Management Journal, 9*(3), 207–223.

Cool, K., Dierickx, I., & Jamison, D. (1989). Business strategy, market structure and risk-return relationships: A structural approach. *Strategic Management Journal, 10*(6), 507–522.

Dichev, I. D., Graham, J. R., Harvey, C. R., & Rajgopal, S. (2013). Earnings quality: Evidence from the field. *Journal of Accounting and Economics, 56*, 1–33.

European Commission. (2007). Internal market, industry, entrepreneurship and SMEs, The six most competitive manufacturing sectors in Europe, 23/11/2007.

Fiegenbaum, A., & Thomas, H. (1986). Dynamic and risk measurement perspectives on Bowman's risk-return paradox for strategic management: An empirical study. *Strategic Management Journal, 7*, 395–407.

McKelvey, B., & Andriani, P. (2005). Why Gaussian statistics are mostly wrong for strategic organization. *Strategic Organization, 3*(2), 219–228.

Nordhaus, W. D. (2011). The economics of tail events with an application to climate change. *Review of Environmental Economics and Policy, 5*(2), 240–257.

Taleb, N. N. (2005). *Fooled by randomness: The hidden role of chance in life and the markets*. New York, NY: Random House (first published in 2001).

Taleb, N. N. (2007). *The Black Swan: The impact of the highly improbable*. New York, NY: Random House.

Taleb, N. N. (2013). *Antifragile: Things that gain from disorder*. London: Penguin Books.

Williams, M. A., Baek, G., Park, L. Y., & Zhao, W. (2016). Global evidence on the distribution of economic profit rates. *Physica A, 458*, 356–363.

Appendix 8.1

Twenty-Three Outliers Comprised by 16 Negative and 7 Positive Outliers

Two Extreme Negative Outliers

1. SQI DIAGNOSTICS INC. (Going concern)

SQI Diagnostics is a Canadian company engaged in the development and commercialization of proprietary technologies and products for use in multiplexing diagnostics. The firm develops multiplexed blood tests that enable simultaneous measurement of molecules like proteins, antibodies, and inflammatory biomarkers. The company is focused on businesses activities in organ transplant, autoimmune disease, and serological testing with a global market outlook although more than half the revenues come from North America (https://sqidiagnostics.com/).

SIC: 3826 Manufacturing materials and machines.
Founded in 1999 with reporting for the years **2010–2019** Avg. ROA = **−121.07**.

Modest asset levels 2010–2019.

3.99	8.75	3.13	4.99	2.98	2.63	2.24	2.91	1.97	2.67	2,773

High negative income 2010–2012.

−3.80	−5.38	−7.10	−4.19	−3.85	−3.13	−2.90	−2.39	−2.94	−3.39	−3.55

Extreme negative ROA.

−95.25	−61.47	−227.02	−83.81	−129.15	−118.93	−129.56	−82.15
−149.12	−127.46	−127.89					

2. SUNRISE TECHNOLOGY INTL. INC. (Bankrupt)

Sunrise Technology is primarily in the business of dental equipment and supplies. Founded by John Pence as he left his job as CIO for an apparel manufacturing company and started Sunrise to solve global supply chain challenges supported by a partnership with Microsoft. The company became insolvent and filed for Chapter 7 bankruptcy in 2002. A large creditor initiated several legal actions that required years of expensive litigation to resolve. In 2007, the remaining assets of Sunrise Technology were acquired by PriaVision, Inc. including the Hyperion® LTK System (https://www.prweb.com/releases/2007/04/prweb522600.htm).

SIC: 3845 Manufacturing materials and machines
Founded in 1994 with reporting for the years **1995–2000** Avg. ROA = **−151.62**

Increasing assets.

6.55	3.54	2.74	10.52	13.31	24.64

Fast increase in losses (negative net income).

−4.04	−5.66	−6.17	−16.34	−23.34	−32.86

Increasing negative ROA.

−61.74	−159.53	−224.42	−155.25	−175.41	−133.38

Fourteen Negative Outliers (ROA < Mean − 4*SD)

3. CHROMADEX CORP. (Going concern)

ChromaDex Corporation based in Los Angeles, California, is a global bioscience company dedicated to healthy aging focused on dietary supplement and food ingredients. The company pioneers research on nicotinamide adenine dinucleotide (NAD+) levels that decline with aging and innovated the NAD+ precursor nicotinamide riboside (NR) commercialized as the ingredient Niagen®. The company stock is publicly traded on NASDAQ (https://investors.chromadex. com/overview/default.aspx).

SIC: 2833 Manufacturing food and apparel.
Founded in 1999 with reporting for the years **2010–2019** Avg. ROA = **−58.86**.

Increasing assets.

4.46	4.17	5.91	5.79	7.43	11.91	12.29	38.24	25.26	23.54

Increasing losses (negative net income).

−1.40	−5.25	−7.63	−2.85	−3.44	−1.76	−1.82	−6.93
−19.93	−18.80						

Increasing negative ROA.

−31.54	−125.92	−129.08	−49.18	−46.42	−14.78	−14.82	−18.14
−78.89	−79.87						

Higher Negative ROA as Losses Increase Faster Than Assets

4. ADVANCED TISSUE SCIENCES INC. (Bankrupt)

A pioneering firm that sold a replacement skin for burn victims and diabetics. The company filed for bankruptcy in 2002 two weeks after the rival, Organogenesis Inc. of Boston, sought bankruptcy protection from its creditors. The bioengineered-skin products even though a scientific achievement was a hard sell in a competitive cost-conscious environment (https://www.latimes.com/ar chives/la-xpm-2002-oct-12-fi-tissue12-story.html).

SIC: 2833 Manufacturing food and apparel.
Started in 1987 with reporting for the years **1995–2001** Avg. ROA = **−55.55**

Increasing assets.

30.49	53.54	47.01	49.50	53.03	51.05	52.67

Increasing losses (negative net income).

−22.64	−21.22	−33.62	−39.69	−19.02	−21.22	−24.13

Increasing negative ROA.

−74.26	−39.65	−71.52	−80.18	−35.88	−41.57	−45.82

Losses Are Increasing Faster Than Assets 1997–1998

5. UNITED ENERGY CORP. (Going concern/Delisted)

United Energy Corporation (UEC) is a diversified oil and gas producer. The company engages in exploration, development, production, technology, and storage of oil and gas reserves. In 2021, UEC announced the purchase of significant assets in the counties of Rogers, Nowata, Osage and Washington, Oklahoma, as well as Montgomery Kansas including oil and gas leases in over 240,000 acres, over 2,200 wells, and 1,200 miles of natural gas pipelines (https://www.unrgcorp.com/).

SIC: 2842 Manufacturing food and apparel.
Reporting from **2002–2010** Avg. ROA = **−98.63**.

Slightly decreasing assets.

0.87	3.01	2.56	1.64	4.50	2.67	1.33	0.65	0.77

Losses (negative net income) retained throughout the period.

−1.14	−2.31	−2.06	−1.44	−3.03	−1.66	−1.44	−0.95	−1.01

High negative ROA.

−131.50	−76.81	−80.51	−87.54	−67.22	−62.20	−107.65
−143.41	−130.80					

Assets increased faster than losses 2002–2003, so ROA dropped (less negative).

6. AMERITYRE CORP. (Going concern)

Amerityre Corporation engages in research and development, manufacturing, and sale of solid polyurethane foam tires. The company's polyurethane material technologies comprise closed-cell polyurethane foam for low-duty cycle applications and Elastothane® with high load-bearing for heavy-duty applications. The company produces polyurethane foam tires for bicycles, golf, and baggage carts, hand trucks, lawn and garden equipment, wheelbarrows, personnel carriers, medical mobility products, and custom designed products (https://amerityre.com/flat-free-tires/mower-tire-size-15x600-6/).

SIC: 3011 Manufacturing materials and machines.
Reporting for the years **2000–2019** Avg. ROA = **−73.05**.

Uneven increase in assets.

1.12	1.57	1.71	3.75	3.22	3.57	4.55	6.37	3.54
2.00	1.75	1,922	1,572	1,497	1,699	1,370	1,171	1,216
1,066	1,608							

Increasing losses (negative net income) then lower until 2016 – profitable in 2017 and 2019.

−1.65	−2.84	−2.11	−2.53	−3.74	−7.78	−3.94	−3.61	−2.90
−2.52	−0.97	-0.560	-0,770	-0,731	-0,801	-0,188	-0,152	0,020
-0,023	0,024	0,020	-0,023	0,024				

High negative ROA in 2000–2002 and 2005–2006.

−148.05	−181.36	−123.46	−67.47	−116.25	−217.70	−86.71	−56.72
−81.94	−126.23	−55.43	−29,14	−48,96	−48,80	−47,12	−13,75
−12,94	1,67	−2,13	1,50				

7. SOLIGEN TECHNOLOGIES INC. (Going concern/Delisted/Restructured)

Soligen Technologies was a provider of casting metal parts and web-based, CAD-driven, cast metal parts production services. Soligen Technologies entered into a Convertible Preferred Stock Purchase Agreement for private placement of shares to 25 private investors in 2001. Under new leadership Soligen Technologies transformed into an environmentally friendly acquisition and oil service company in 2018 (https://www.soligen.com/).

SIC: 3360 Manufacturing materials and machines.
Founded in 1988 with reporting for the years **1995–2000** Avg. ROA = **−55.20**.

Steady level of assets.

3.07	2.42	2.39	1.84	2.17	2.09

Losses (negative net income) decreasing slightly.

−2.09	−1.40	−0.89	−1.56	−0.79	−0.95

High but slightly decreasing negative ROA.

−68.34	−57.83	−37.57	−85.09	−36.76	−45.62

8. DISC INC. (Going concern/Delisted)

Disc, Inc. is a premier service provider of digitizing vintage media to digital. Delisted from the NASDAQ SmallCap Market in 2003 (https://www.sec.gov/Archives/edga r/data/891788/000089161803003368/f91172e8vk.htm).

SIC: 3572 Manufacturing materials and machines.
Established in 1982 with reporting for the years **1995–2002** Avg. ROA = **−62.91**.

Increasing level of assets particularly in last years 2001–2002.

3.70	3.89	3.86	4.55	4.32	3.36	11.47	8.95

Increasing level of losses (negative net income).

−2.77	−3.17	−2.32	−2.05	−1.84	−3.40	−4.50	−5.29

Dip in assets, increase in losses – higher negative ROA in 2000.

−74.74	−81.31	−60.06	−44.97	−42.47	−101.36	−39.27	−59.05

9. ANCOR COMMUNICATIONS INC. (Delisted/Acquired)

Ancor Communications Inc. was primarily operating in the business of manufacturing network switches and computer communications equipment. The company was acquired in May 2000 for $1.7 billion by QLogic Corp. based in by Aliso Viejo, California (https://money.cnn.com/2000/05/08/deals/qlogic/).

SIC: 3576 Manufacturing materials and machines.
Reporting for the years **1995–1999** (delisted) Avg. ROA = **−63.86**.

Sharp increase in assets in 1999.

5.65	11.62	9.47	11.68	86.15

Volatile loss development.

−3.20	−5.01	−9.15	−13.29	−7.79

High negative ROA dropping in 1999 as assets increase.

−56.63	−43.14	−96.65	−113.82	−9.05

10. C-PHONE CORP. (Delisted)

C-phone Corp was primarily in the business of telephone and telegraph apparatus. Delisting from Nasdaq SmallCap Market with F-15 termination of registration with the SEC in 2001 (https://www.sec.gov/rules/final/34-52029.pdf).

SIC: 3360 Manufacturing materials and machines North Carolina.
Incorporated in 1993 with reporting for the years **1995–1999** Avg. ROA = **−79.55**.

Steady level of assets slightly down.

6.05	3.43	6.00	5.71	3.52

Losses all along.

−4.03	−2.83	−5.54	−4.09	−2.98

Very negative ROA.

−66.70	−82.41	−92.36	−71.62	−84.63

11. ARIEL CORP. (Delisted/Going concern)

Ariel Corp. is a large manufacturer of separable reciprocating gas compressors for worldwide customers used in the global energy industry to extract, process, transport, store, and distribute natural gas from the wellhead to the end-user. In 2001, Karen Buchwald Wright, the daughter of the founder Jim Buchwald, assumed the presidency of the company (https://www.arielc orp.com/compressors/compressor-landing-page.html).

SIC: 3372 Manufacturing materials and machines.
Since 1966 with reporting for the years **1995–2001** Avg. ROA = **−62.12**.

Increasing then dropping level of assets.

18.53	19.05	10.36	30.88	17.69	7.95

Net income increasingly negative.

−3.15	−8.34	−11.89	11.07	−11.16	−13.51

Negative ROA increasing sharply as assets drop.

−17.02	−43.78	−114.74	35.86	−63.08	−169.94

12. DIASYS CORP. (Delisted/Going concern)

DiaSys Diagnostic Systems was a specialist in development and manufacturing of diagnostic system solutions. The company faced liquidity problems in 2004 engaging in a private loan agreement with changes in ownership control. It was delisted in 2008. In 2016, the veterinary division of US-based DiaSys Diagnostic Systems announced its next-generation, fully integrated respons®920VET clinical chemistry analyzer (https://www.diasys-us.com/).

SIC: 3826 Manufacturing materials and machines.
Founded in 1992 with reporting for the years **1995–2008** Avg. ROA = **−49.95**.

Steadily dropping level of assets.

4.24	3.11	1.76	2.53	1.60	3.23	4.82	4.16	3.57
2.66	2.15	1.828	1,796					

Losses vary but at steady level.

−0.65	−0.99	−1.88	−1.82	−0.96	−0.82	−1.49	−1.37	−1.32
−2.36	−1.56	-0.776	-0,566					

ROA at varied but high negative levels.

−15.28	−32.04	−107.05	−72.12	−60.53	−25.52	−31.00
−32.94	−37.09	−88.84	−72.91	-42,46	-31,54	

13. BIOJECT MEDICAL TECHNOLOGIES (Delisted/Acquired)

Bioject Medical Technologies delivered devices for liquid medication through tiny pores in the human skin creating an ultra-fine stream of high-pressure fluid. It makes needle-free injection devices for intramuscular and subcutaneous injections. The company was acquired by Inovio Pharmaceuticals in 201 (https://www.crunchbase.com/acquisition/inovio-pharmaceuticals-acquires-bioject-medical-technologies-9e588cec).

SIC: 3841 Manufacturing materials and machines.
Reporting from **1995–2010** (delisting) Avg. ROA = **−55.46**.

Increasing but volatile asset levels.

7.25	6.65	6.46	7.82	8.61	15.34	28.13	23.45	18.32
14.51	10.65	7,913	5,703	4,144	3,658	2,517		

Net income is always negative but decreasingly so.

−5.24	−4.03	−15.30	−5.16	−1.68	−4.16	−5.02	−4.54	−7.61
−7.17	−5.03	-5,211	-2,890	-2,176	-0,751	-1,011		

Relatively high negative ROA throughout.

−72.23	−60.61	−236.70	−65.93	−19.53	−27.11	−17.84
−19.36	−41.53	−49.43	−47.25	-65,86	-50,67	-52,51
-20,53	-40,19					

14. VIDAMED INC. (Delisted/Acquired)

Vidamed Inc. was a developer of treatments for urological disorders. Its primary product was Vidamed Tuna System offering a less invasive treatment of symptoms for benign prostatic hyperplasia or enlarged prostate. The company was acquired by Minneapolis-based Medtronic (https://www.nytimes.com/2001/12/07/business/company-news-medtronic-to-buy-vidamed-for-326-million.html).

SIC: 3841 Manufacturing materials and machines.
Founded in 1992 with reporting for the years **1995–2002** Avg. ROA = **−99.03**

Volatile asset levels.

18.42	12.17	15.81	12.96	6.53	16.75	14.99

Slightly decreasing losses (negative net income).

−14.55	−12.83	−15.34	−18.22	−10.63	−9.20	−8.03

Extremely high negative ROA in periods.

−78.96	−105.42	−97.08	−140.62	−162.58	−54.96	−53.58

15. CARDIODYNAMICS INTL. CORP. (Delisted/Acquired)

Cardiodynamics International Corp. is primarily engaged in development and manufacturing of electro-medical and electrotherapeutic apparatus. The company was acquired by SonoSite, Inc. (a leading company in hand-carried and point-of-care ultrasound) in 2009 (https://www.sonosite.com/blog/sonosite-completes-acquisition-cardiodynamics-cardiovascular-disease-management-company).

SIC: 3845 Manufacturing materials and machines.
Reporting from **1995–2010** (delisting) Avg. ROA = **−65.80**.

Increasing level of assets.

0.76	1.39	3.74	4.26	7.59	18.61	18.18	19.54	21.71
45.66	30.42	27.142	14,207	11,014				

Net income mostly negative throughout and increasing.

−2.35	−2.38	−3.98	−4.89	−3.56	−7.13	−0.56	0.26
1.99	7.96	−11.37	-4.993	-11,942	-2,278		

ROA extremely negative in the beginning.

−308.34	−170.82	−106.34	−114.76	−46.99	−38.34	−3.07	1.32
9.20	17.44	−37.36	-18,40	-84,05	-20,68		

16. INNOVATIVE GAMING CORP. (Bankrupt/Acquired)

The Innovation Gaming Group was a provider of gaming technology as a member of the organization of innovative gaming technology companies and casino advisory operator. The company went into bankruptcy in 2001 and all its assets were sold to Xertain, Inc., a privately held Las Vegas-based gaming technology company (https://lasvegassun.com/news/2000/feb/07/innovative-gaming-sells-assets/).

SIC: 3990 Manufacturing materials and machines.
Reporting from **1995–2002** (delisting) Avg. ROA = **−55.36**.

Decreasing level of assets.

18.53	15.14	17.87	15.67	7.19	9.58	7.94

Negative net income – increasing losses.

−2.07	−5.85	−1.80	−3.98	−11.49	−0.64	−10.78

ROA extremely negative in 1999 as assets decrease and losses increase.

−11.17	−38.68	−10.09	−25.38	−159.79	−6.69	−135.75

Six–Seven Positive Outliers (ROA > Mean – 4*sd)

17. GRACO INC. (Going concern)

Graco Inc. is located in Minneapolis, Minnesota. The company designs, manu-factures, and markets thousands of fluid handling products and solutions for the manufacturing, processing, construction and maintenance industries around the world. The firm provides technologies and expertise to manage fluids and coat-ings in industrial and commercial applications. It markets systems and equipment to move, measure, control, dispense and spray fluid and powder materials (https://www.graco.com/us/en/homeowner/product/17g177-magnum-prox17.html).

SIC: 3561 Manufacturing materials and machines.
Reporting for the years **1995–2019** Avg. ROA = **+19.98**.

Relatively steady increase in assets.

213.31	234.82	246.57	214.38	210.81	205.62	234.94	295.72	324.17
293.63	340.31	381,0	384,1	414,6	331,6	363,8	582,3	865,2
856,0	988,8	884,1	773,9	840,9	881,1	989,7		

Steadily increasing profits.

27.16	34.31	41.73	43.37	53.04	60.61	55.52	62.83	70.75	85.82
96.13	111,5	109,4	86,4	34,1	70,5	94,8	97,6	136,0	144,4
219,7	25,3	153,9	204,0	201,1					

High slightly volatile ROA at high levels.

12.72	14.60	16.90	20.22	25.14	29.46	23.64	21.25	21.82	29.24
28.24	29,27	28,48	20,85	10,28	19,39	16,28	11,28	15,88	14,60
24,85	3,27	18,30	23,16	20,32					

18. ARMANINO FOODS DISTINCTION (Going concern)

Armanino Foods Distinction is a California-based company producing upscale frozen and refrigerated Italian-style foods. The company's flagship product is pesto that it makes half a dozen varieties. The firm also manufactures frozen filled pastas and frozen meatballs (https://armaninofoods.com/).

SIC: 2230 Manufacturing foods and apparel.
Started in 1978 and incorporated in 1986 with reporting for the years **1995–2019** Avg. ROA = **+14.98**.

Relatively steady decrease in assets – high to begin with then slightly decreasing.

8.86	11.30	12.05	10.13	10.08	8.67	9.16	7.25	6.90
6.54	6.39	5.879	5,788	4,944	5,426	5,877	6,145	6,144
7,046	8,068	9,039	9,432	13,588	15,137	16,694		

Steady profits (one year loss) then steadily increasing profits toward 2019.

1.07	0.42	0.67	0.20	0.45	0.66	0.54	-0.32	0.22	0.25
0.49	0.599	0,654	0,496	1,093	1,582	1,593	1,891	2,146	2,462
2,562	2,631	3,101	3,749	3,793					

Steady to steadily increasing ROAs.

12.07	3.75	5.54	1.97	4.52	7.60	5.90	−4.48	3.18	3.80
7.74	10,18	11,30	10,04	20,15	26,92	25,92	30,78	30,46	30,52
28,34	27,89	22,82	24,76	22,72					

19. UNITED-GUARDIAN INC. (Going concern)

United-Guardian is a diversified company that conducts research and product development of proprietary industrial products as well as manufacturing and marketing of cosmetic ingredients, pharmaceuticals, medical, and healthcare products (https://u-g.com/).

SIC: 2834 Manufacturing foods and apparel.
Started in 1942 with reporting for the years **1995–2019** Avg. ROA = **+21.83**.

Relatively steady increase in assets throughout but dropping from 2010 onwards.

5.79	5.55	5.71	6.23	7.05	8.12	9.17	9.73	11.44
11.39	11.47	11.875	12,189	12,357	13,026	9,652	10,161	9,072
10,094	10,202	9,969	9,412	7,836	7,505	7,231		

Steadily increasing profits toward 2019.

0.27	0.49	0.76	0.93	1.24	1.77	1.61	1.18	2.01	1.95
1.99	2.039	2,536	2,261	2,700	2,606	3,142	3,162	3,807	2,592
2,928	1,607	2,344	2,604	2,785					

Steady and then steadily increasing ROAs.

4.61	9.00	13.45	14.92	17.61	21.85	17.54	12.15	17.62	17.16
17.42	17,17	20,81	18,30	20,73	27,00	30,92	34,86	37,72	25,41
29,37	17,07	29,91	34,69	38,52					

20. LOTUS PHARMACEUTICALS INC. (Delisted)

Lotus is the largest pharmaceutical company in Taiwan with a primary focus on high-value generic products in the fields of central nervous system (CNS), cardiovascular system (CVS), oncology, women's health, and anti-obesity drugs in tablet form and as hard and softgel capsules to the global markets (https://www.lotuspharm.com/company).

SIC: 2834 Manufacturing foods and apparel listed on Taiwan Stock Exchange. Founded in 1966 with reporting for the years **2006–2010** (why only periodic reporting?) Avg. ROA = **+20.60**.

Dramatic increase in assets from 2006 onwards.

16.19	26.40	45.55	58.73	70.76

Profits (net income) tripled toward 2010.

3.08	803	9.15	11.44	9.89

High-level ROA.

19.06	30.40	20.08	19.47	13.98

21. WD-40 CO (Going concern)

WD-40 is based in San Diego, California, and was originally known as the Rocket Chemical Company. The company is a manufacturer of household and multi-use products including the signature brand, WD-40. Other recognized brands include 3-In-One Oil, Lava, Spot Shot, X-14, Carpet Fresh, GT85, 1001, Solvol, 2000 Flushes, and No Vac (https://wd40.dk/).

SIC: 2890 Manufacturing foods and apparel
Reporting from the years **1995–2019** Avg. ROA = **+16.86**

Steady increase in assets.

58.57	58.91	61.15	65.26	82.71	73.89	141.10	178.87	192.69
187.80	194.57	197,90	204,71	185,69	182,88	199,04	185,62	196,29
207,62	219,70	213,96	211,97	226,33	188,99	177,31		

Steadily increasing profits (net income).

20.11	20.35	19.97	20.13	19.85	17.88	13.47	20.52	23.32	20.34
21.27	20,72	22,80	18,95	18,31	24,85	24,17	23,15	25,59	27,64
28,26	32,84	32,40	38,87	32,75					

Slightly declining ROA but retained at high level.

34.33	34.54	32.66	30.85	23.99	24,20	9.54	11,47	12,10	10,83
10.93	10,47	11,14	10,20	10,01	12,48	13,02	11,79	12,32	12,58
13,21	15,49	14,32	20,57	18,47					

22. VITREOUS GLASS INC. (Going concern)

Vitreous Glass is located in Airdrie, Alberta, Canada, and is a part of the waste treatment and disposal industry. Vitreous removes the various contaminates in glass and crushes the wasted glass to sand grains. The resulting product Glas-Sand™ is then sold to fiberglass insulation manufacturers as furnace ready cullet to be used in their production facilities (https://www.vitreousglass.ca/).

SIC: 3220 Manufacturing materials and machines.
Started in 1995 with reporting for the years **2013–2019** Avg. ROA = **+32.68**.

Slight decline in asset level.

3.86	3.78	3.06	2.75	2.73	2.52	2.16

Slightly increasing profits (net income).

0.85	1.16	0.94	0.99	0.95	0.97	0.78

Slight increase in **ROA**.

22.00	30.61	30.67	36.15	34.80	38.43	36.11

23. WATERFURNACE RENEWABLE ENERGY (Acquired)

Geothermal produces geothermal heat pumps for efficient and effective all-year-round operations to use the CO_2 neutral and infinite energy source within the earth.

In 2014, WaterFurnace was acquired by NIBE, a leading heat pump manufacturer for the European market (https://www.nibe.com/investors/pm-news-acquisitions-other/2014-news-acquisitions-other/2014-08-22-nibe-completes-acquisition-of-waterfurnace).

SIC: 3433 Manufacturing materials and machines.
Reporting from **2000–2013** (acquired) Avg. ROA = **+18.38**.

Steady increase in assets.

14.44	18.75	19.01	18.94	20.09	22.28	25.11	24.74	34.03	35.78
40.99	45,35	46,35	50,26						

Initial loss, then creasing profits (net income tripling).

−3.15	3.31	3.18	3.03	3.69	4.61	6.27	6.78	10.89
10.68	9.49	9.197	6,627	8,887				

Steady high **ROA**.

−21.82	17.67	16.74	16.03	18.36	20.71	24.97	27.43	32.02
29.86	23.15	20,28	14,30	17,68				

Chapter 9

Summary and Conclusion

Abstract

This chapter outlines the major analytical efforts performed as part of the overarching research project with the aim to investigate the organizational and environmental circumstances around the extreme negatively skewed performance outcomes regularly observed across firms. It presents the collection and treatment of comprehensive European and North American datasets where subsequent analyses reproduce the contours of performance distributions observed in prior empirical studies. Key theoretical perspectives engaged in prior studies of performance data and the implied risk-return relationships are presented and these point to emerging commonalities between empirical findings in the management and finance fields. The results from extended analyses of more fine-grained data from North American manufacturing firms uncover the subtle effects of leadership and structural features, and computational simulations demonstrate how the implied adaptive processes can lead to the empirically observed performance distributions. Finally, the findings from the analytical project activities are set in context and the implications of the observed results are discussed to reach at a final conclusion.

Keywords: Leadership traits; left-skewed performance distributions; high excess kurtosis; negative risk-return relationship; rapid environmental changes; strategic adaptation

Introduction

The preceding chapters present the sequential development of analytical undertakings as part of a broader research project intended to come to grips with the observed fat-tailed performance distributions where many firms seem to underperform and only few excel (e.g., Bloom & Van Reenen, 2007). These efforts were intended to ascertain if the observed empirical artifacts are reproduced in

A Study of Risky Business Outcomes: Adapting to Strategic Disruption, 143–158
Copyright © 2023 by Torben Juul Andersen
Published under exclusive licence by Emerald Publishing Limited
doi:10.1108/978-1-83797-074-220231009

large updated datasets and, if so, to form a better understanding of how these outcomes may derive from the ability of firms to deal with rapid environmental changes (e.g., Teece, 2007) where many firms appear to end up in a left tail of underperformers.

The project collected extensive datasets on European and North American firms over the 25-year period 1995–2019 that spans episodic business scenarios of global expansion, economic recession, and recovery up until the effects from the COVID-19 crisis emerged in late 2020. The analyses of both datasets consistently uncover the extreme left-skewed performance distributions with small positive tails of high performers across the geographical regions, different industry segments, and periodic economic scenarios with diverse competitive conditions (Albæk & Andersen, 2021). Refined analyses of the datasets find that the left-skewed return distributions are associated with negative risk-return relationships, where high performers generate superior returns with less variation in outcomes (e.g., Andersen & Bettis, 2015; Bowman, 1980; Bromiley, 1991; Nickel & Rodriques, 2001). These favorable risk-return outcomes appear deflated by over-confident executives and low flexibility in capital deployment for opportunistic investment.

Flexibility and openness to interpret and respond to rapidly changing business contexts seem paramount for successful organizational maneuvering in dynamic complex environments where extreme events may arise that are difficult to predict and foresee (e.g., Van der Vegt et al., 2015). The human reaction to the unpleasant feeling of uncertainty is often to adopt control-based management practices in a belief that it will contain the incertitude that surrounds the organization. While central analytical thinking is advantageous, the adoption of central (diagnostic) controls is typically not the proper answer because it tends to stifle the ability to respond and adapt where open interactive decision-making processes seem to facilitate effective adaptation to disruptive incidents (Van der Vegt et al., 2015).

Strategic adaptation is not a new concept (e.g., Andersen, 2015), but it is of increasing relevance in disruptive environments that display the so-called high-velocity conditions (e.g., Eisenhardt, 1989). The global business context is arguably more exposed to improbable extreme and often unexpected events than we normally perceive (e.g., Taleb, 2007). These events include technology leaps and industrial paradigm shifts (e.g., Lasi et al., 2014) and high-impact low-probability natural phenomena (e.g., Meyer & Kunreuther, 2017). Such disruptive incidents can change the advantages and superiority of existing (optimal) practices in ways that create significant strategic discontinuities across the competitive landscape. In these complex dynamic contexts girded with potentially extreme unpredictable incidents, contingency planning is difficult, and it is hard to identify risks and plan responses in advance (e.g., Andersen & Schrøder, 2010). As a consequence, even large established firms can lose their dominant market positions where past evidence suggests that close to half of Fortune 500 companies may disappear from the list over 10–15 years (e.g., Goodburn, 2015). Extreme developments like these may account for firms that move toward the negative left tail of the performance distribution where better strategic adaptation might circumvent such a fate. So honing in on the dynamic processes that can enhance the adaptive capacity of organizations under erratic and changing conditions seems a worthwhile exercise.

The ability to practice good management skills and consistently demonstrate effective adaptive responses should secure a steady stream of profits reflected in high financial returns captured by the so-called "Bowman paradox" where high average returns associate with low variance in returns (Bowman, 1980). The implied negative relationship between risk and performance, and vice versa, appears to be a real empirical artifact (e.g., Bromiley, 1991) and it seems linked to the left-skewed performance distribution (Henkel, 2009). These phenomena can also be shaped by outcomes from diverse organizational adaptation processes across competing firms as they face rapid environmental changes (e.g., Andersen et al., 2007). Hence, if some (or even a few) of the firms have superior response capabilities, the adaptive processes will form left-skewed performance distributions where many firms show adverse outcomes and negative relationships between conventional risk and return measures (Andersen & Bettis, 2014, 2015).

A common observation from realized performance data is that a vast number of firms perform relatively poorly as expressed in a left-skewed tail of underperformers with some outliers showing extreme negative returns. The negatively skewed performance distributions have strong leptokurtic features that often violate the assumed normality of the data as a perquisite for the application of many conventional statistical methods. To accommodate these restrictions in sampled data, mainstream studies often apply automated screening processes and standard winsorization techniques to identify extreme values for deletion or transformation (e.g., Boisot & McKelvey, 2011). These practices tend to rid the outliers from analysis and thereby make it impossible to uncover insights that otherwise could be hidden in the empirical evidence observed around outlier cases in the negative and positive tails of performance distributions.

As part of the project progression, we extracted comprehensive updated datasets to investigate the predominance and persistency of empirically observed left-skewed performance distributions and negative risk-return relationships. Based on prior literature streams in the management and finance fields, we considered ways of testing earlier empirical findings, identify effects of structural and behavioral traits while challenging some of the underlying assumptions and methodological practices. We conducted exploratory simulation studies based on representative strategic response models and uncovered outcomes that resemble the empirically observed performance data. Finally, we identified specific negative and positive performance outliers and generated new interesting insights that help us (better) understand why some organizations end up in the extreme tails and possible links to adaptive capabilities.

Altogether, these efforts have provided (some) evidence that can help us understand what causes differences in outcomes commonly expressed in extreme left-skewed performance distributions. In this way, we have refined our ability to explain, or at least better understand how hitherto unexplained empirical regularities observed in realized performance data arise (Helfat, 2007), including influences of organizational artifacts and environmental conditions on outcomes and the eventual performance distribution.

General Development

We wanted to investigate the circumstances that lead to extreme left-skewed performance distributions and with this to understand how strategic adaptation may affect the observed performance outcomes and thereby eventually help organizations refine their adaptive processes and improve performance. The associated inverse risk-return relationships have been studied based of different rationales in empirical research efforts including the psychological and behavioral aspects of decision-makers, spurious statistical effects, and diverse dynamic capabilities among firms. The theoretical underpinnings and specific methodologies applied in these studies of the risk-return phenomena have been largely disjointed constituting distinct research streams with little interaction and limited awareness, or recognition of each other. In this project, we attempted to look across these rather secluded fields of study.

Sampling the Data

We collected two comprehensive datasets for North American and European firms from the Compustat databases comprising a number of variables that enable further analysis of different performance ratios, notably return on assets (financial return) as the norm for management studies (see Chapter 2). Other performance ratios, for example, cash flow return and Tobin's q were derived as well for robustness checks as well as other variables to assess influences of basic executive behaviors and structural dimensions. Collecting annual data points to measure multiple variables for all firms extending over a 25-year period (1995–2019) will encounter numerous discrepancies in reported values and empty data cells with missing values. In other words, there is a need to "clean" the data for possible misspecifications and consider alternative ways to treat the missing value issue. We did this in various ways. First, we dropped firms with more than 50% missing values in one of the years reasoning that indicates "sloppy" reporting of the values that we cannot rely on. Second, extreme values that clearly appeared excessive in terms of their absolute size, or because they fail to comply with basic accounting rules, were replaced by an empty data cell and thereafter treated like a missing value. Third, we treated the missing variables in accordance with three alternative methods including the complete case, multiple imputation (MICE), and K-nearest neighbor (KNN) approaches. We show that the KNN approach generates data that most closely resemble the original datasets, whereas the complete case, which is the commonly used approach in management studies eliminates a substantial number of outliers from the sample.

Analyses of the distribution characteristics identified by the skewness and kurtosis measures on financial returns of all firms over the 25-year period generally revealed negatively skewed distributions with high excess kurtosis way beyond the values assumed in normally distributed data (see Chapter 3). Of the applied data treatments to deal with missing values, the complete case approach results in the lowest negative skewness and excess kurtosis, whereas the MICE approach generates even more extreme values, while the KNN approach is close to reproduce the distribution characteristics of the original sample. With respect to number of firms in the dataset, the complete case reduces the sample size by around 70% of all the firms in the original dataset, whereas the KNN approach retains almost all firms. Looking at the number of outliers (defined by firms with ROA below the first quartile minus 1.5 times the difference between the first and third quartile, the interquartile range, and firms above the third quartile plus 1.5 times the interquartile range) we observe that the complete case sample has around 9–14% of outliers across industries, whereas the KNN dataset varies within 10–18%. That is, even though the complete case data are more than halved in number of observations there is still a substantial share of outliers in the dataset. If we consider extreme outliers (defined by firms with ROA below the first quartile minus 3.0 times the difference between the first and third quartile and firms above the third quartile plus 3.0 times the interquartile range) we observe around 4–9% of extreme outliers in the complete case sample, whereas the KNN dataset has around 5–12%. In other words, there (also) remains a substantial share of extreme outliers in the vastly reduced complete case sample.

Extended analyses of the complete case datasets show pervasive negative skewness and excess kurtosis across all industry segment (SIC Divisions) with substantial percentages of outliers as well as extreme outliers although somewhat less so than the original samples (see Chapter 4). When plotting the frequency distributions of ROA (return on assets) for all firms throughout the 25-year period in each of the industry segments, we observe the contours of extreme left-skewed distributions with many outliers (negative and positive). That is, the negative kurtosis is not generated by one, or just a few, extreme outliers but is caused by a rather pervasive presence of a rather large number of firms posting negative financial returns. Considering the distributions of financial return (ROA) over shorter five-year intervals within the 25-year sampling period, we observe similarly left-skewed distribution outcomes. Looking specifically on firms operating in manufacturing industries (SIC: 3000–3999), which has been used as a sampling basis in many empirical studies, we see predominantly left-skewed distributions (Fig. 9.1). Yet, we note some differences between the North American and European datasets over time where the European data, with a shorter less-developed history, show positively skewed return distributions in the earlier periods 1995–1999, 2000–2004, and 2005–2009. However, both the North American and European datasets show extreme negatively skewed performance distributions in the subsequent time-intervals 2010–2014 and 2015–2019 reflecting competitive conditions around a global financial crisis and subsequent economic recovery.

Theoretical Foundations

The interest in performance outcomes and their eventual distributions have been the topic of numerous studies in the management and finance fields (see Chapter 5). The two fields of study have generally adopted somewhat different approaches in the underlying analyses of these phenomena. Studies in the management field typically consider realized performance outcomes as determined by accounting-based return measures, whereas finance studies typically consider market-based

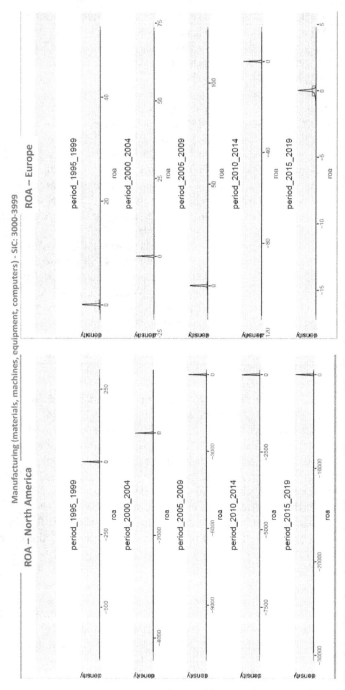

Fig. 9.1.   Plotting the Density Diagrams (Frequency Distributions) of Returns Across Manufacturing Firms.

Note: Performance data = Return on Assets (ROA), Complete Case datasets

returns that integrate investor expectations about the firm's future earnings potential. Despite the different starting points several commonalities appear to emerge from the empirical studies in the two fields, such as, frequently observed negatively skewed leptokurtic performance outcomes with high excess kurtosis and inverse risk-return relationships, or at least failure to definitively confirm positive risk-return relations.

The management literature has generally observed extreme events associated with largely left-skewed performance distributions that tend to inflict adverse risk outcomes and inverse risk-return relationships (e.g., Nordhaus, 2011; Santacruz, 2019; Taleb, 2007). Various studies have examined the negative relationship between financial returns and performance risk based on behavioral and cognitive rationales (e.g., Bowman, 1980, 1981; Fiegenbaum & Thomas, 1986, 1988). It has been argued that inverse risk-return calculations are caused by statistical artifacts (e.g., Ruefli, 1990; Ruefli & Wiggens, 1994) where left-skewed distributions impose negative risk-returns relations (Henkel, 2000, 2009). Nonetheless, many empirical studies have produced the negative risk-return relationships even when applying different methodologies and construct measures (e.g., Bromiley, 1991; McNamara & Bromiley, 1997, 1999; Santacruz, 2019). The concepts of strategic response capabilities (Bettis & Hitt, 1995), dynamic capabilities (Teece et al., 1997), and dynamic managerial capabilities (Adner & Helfat, 2003) draw attention to outcome effects associated with the ability to manage strategic adaptation in turbulent environments. These adaptive processes can be modeled as strategic responsiveness that captures different aptness in observing emergent change, taking adaptive responses, and thereby gaining a good fit with the competitive environment (e.g., Andersen et al., 2007).

The finance literature has over time questioned predominant assumptions about log-normal returns and positive risk-return relations in a number of empirical studies based on comprehensive historical datasets as well as ex ante assessment by professional investment managers (e.g., Fama & French, 1992, 2000; Shefrin, 2007, 2014). Yet, the implied assumptions about higher required rate of return on more risky investments, as reflected in the capital asset pricing model (CAPM), remains a predominant approach in contemporary financial management. Some dynamic studies of stock market returns find indications of negative relationships between stock returns and price volatility as an indicator of risk (e.g., Campbell & Hentschel, 1992; Conrad et al., 2013; Duffee, 1995). The inverse risk-return relations have been linked to business conditions (Alles & Kling, 1994), executive stock options (Ekholm & Pasternack, 2005), and biases in investment assessments (Shefrin, 2007) identifying competitive, managerial, and executive effects also noted in the management literature. We further discern a development toward up-front management of firm-specific risks (e.g., Froot et al., 1993; Nocco & Stultz, 2006), which previously was considered irrelevant because they could be diversified away in invested portfolios. The left-skewed return distribution and heavy-tailed leptokurtic outcomes have been associated with short-lived firms (Dichev, Graham, Harvey, & Rajgopal, 2013).

Analyzing the Data

We conducted more detailed studies based on the complete case data collected for all firms operating in the North American manufacturing industries, a sector that has been subject to many prior studies, to reexamine earlier findings based on the new updated sample (see Chapter 6). In this examination, we considered possible relationships between the numerator and denominator variables that make up the ratio-based return measure (ROA) and found that they follow vastly different distributions. Net income follows a positively skewed high kurtosis distribution, whereas total assets display a power-law distribution with many small firms and few very large companies that when put together form the negatively skewed high kurtosis return (ROA) distribution. We also reproduced the inverse risk-return relationships with return measured as average ROA correlated against the standard deviation in ROA as risk indicator (e.g., Andersen et al., 2007; Bowman, 1980; Bromiley, 1991). As previous studies found a direct relationship between left-skewed distributions and the negative average-variation relationships (e.g., Henkel, 2000, 2009), we tested the same relationships based on the net income data that constitute positively skewed performance outcomes and therefore should not be subsumed into this automatic inverse relationship. Here we observed that the negative risk-return relationships were miniscule based on the full cross-sectoral data sample, whereas significant and substantive negative risk-return correlations reemerged in the specific industry samples. In other words, there appears to be an underlying adaptive dynamic at play among firms that compete under the same environmental conditions that will lead to the inverse risk-return relationship.

We further considered possible mediating effects on the observed inverse risk-return relationships from executive overconfidence (e.g., Schrand & Zechman, 2012; Schumacher et al., 2020), incentives to manipulate the accounts (Di Meoa et al., 2017; Gunny, 2010), and structural flexibilities like cash holdings and investment autonomy. These possible influences were assessed in split sample comparisons between below and above mean subsamples, where the ROA distributions were positively skewed in the high-performance sample and negatively skewed in the under-performing sample. The above mean subsample showed significantly lower executive overconfidence and significantly higher incentives to manipulate accounts and higher investment autonomy compared to the low-performing subsample. This confirms our expectations that leadership traits and organizational structure exert important influences on the risk-return relations and that we should control for effects of accounting manipulation. These relationships could also be analyzed in conventional multiple regression analysis using alternative performance measures for robustness tests and controlling for potential confounding influences (Fig. 9.2). When applying the regression approach one should obviously be extremely cautious about potential outlier effects where proper analysis of the potential outlier firms is necessary.

These findings are largely consistent with results uncovered from the extant management literature where we as something new specifically identify influences from accounting manipulation and leadership traits in decision-making processes and structural features (Ditchev & Tang, 2009). We find positively skewed accounting

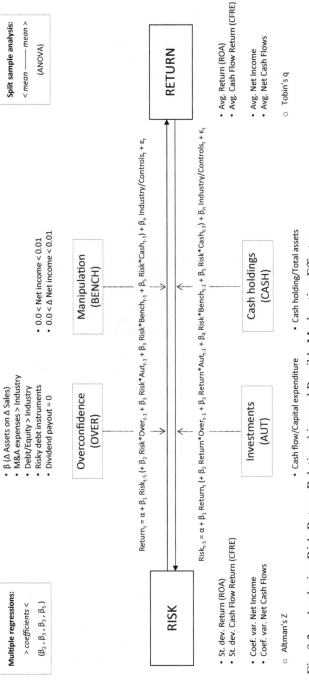

Fig. 9.2. Analyzing Risk-Return Relationships and Possible Moderating Effects.

returns among high performers and negatively skewed returns among low performers. Superior accounting performance is associated with incentives to manipulate earnings and the flexibility of investment autonomy. Underperformance is significantly associated with executive overconfidence and higher bankruptcy risk measured by Altman's Z. The inverse risk-return relationships are found particularly prevalent in sub-industries, where firms are exposed to similar competitive conditions and in periods of economic growth where competition is more intense. Interestingly, we find that Tobin's q, a market-based performance indicator, only is marginally better in the high-performance sample compared to the low-performance sample, and that Tobin's q among the 100 lowest performers is surprisingly high suggesting that the extreme underperformers still represent a high future earnings potential.

Alternative Simulations

We then considered whether alternative strategic responsiveness models could provide viable explanation for the empirically observed performance distributions and risk outcomes found in the large sample of firms operating in the North American manufacturing industries (see Chapter 7). Here the rationale is that as firms attempt to deal with uncertain and unpredictable changes in the competitive landscape, they display different response capabilities where those that adapt well generate higher and steady performance developments commensurate with inverse risk-return relations (e.g., Andersen, 2021; Andersen & Bettis, 2014, 2015; Andersen et al., 2007). That is, if a firm practices effective strategic adaptation it leads to steady performance outcomes at a higher performance level over time. The strategic responsiveness model was formalized in a mathematical performance function that we then programmed to run computational simulations for different adaptive processes and environmental contexts to assess the effects on associated performance distributions and risk-return relationships.

Computational simulation outcomes from different versions of the strategic responsiveness model generate negatively skewed, excess kurtosis, performance distributions with many negative outliers and some positive outliers, although producing fewer positive outliers compared to the empirical data. The simulations consider different competitive contexts and their effects on outcomes including the consequences of periodic incidents of different high-impact low-probability events. The results show that variability in returns is higher in intensely competitive periods compared to scenarios with periodic crises and recovery. The competitive intensity is reflected in the responsiveness model by an exponential parameter that inflicts exponentially higher mismatch effects on performance outcomes and thereby generates more left-skewed performance outcomes with higher inverse risk-return relationships. The model programs adaptation as a learning process where the firm can update its knowledge about the environment over time year by year, or quarter by quarter. So, learning is a discretionary parameter expressed in a learning rate that increases the learning effort but also incurs related learning and adaptation costs. Hence, there is a trade-off between improved knowledge and the costs derived from the learning process and subsequent adaptive use of the acquired knowledge. We find that lower learning rates are optimal when the learning and adaptation costs increase. That is, complete learning in a rapidly changing business context is not optimal when it relates to costly processes.

The analysis compares the effects of adopting two different adaptation approaches of central planning that follows annual budget controls and interactive updating where information is updated more frequently on a quarterly basis through ongoing budget follow-up discussions. The relative effects of the alternative strategic adaptation approaches are not obvious. More frequent updating provides more accurate market intelligence but also generates higher expenses from more intense information-processing activities. Nonetheless, the simulations generally show how (more) frequent strategic updating improves effective adaptation and leads to less negatively skewed distribution with lower excess kurtosis. However, these outcomes do not coincide with the performance outcomes observed in the empirical data, so most firms appear more inclined toward the central planning approach that generates more left-skewed distributions.

The simulation outcomes from the strategic responsiveness model are found to generate left-skewed performance outcomes with many extreme negative outliers and a few positive outliers while displaying negative risk-return relations as observed in the empirical data. Hence, the analyses demonstrate how negatively skewed performance distributions and inverse risk-return relationships can derive from different adaptive processes among competing firms.

Analyzing Outliers

Firms with outlier performance outcomes are generally given a blind eye and eliminated in most mainstream management studies to obtain convenient Gaussian properties in the collected data (e.g., Boisot & McKelvey, 2011). Therefore, we made it a point in this project to identify the firms with extreme negative and positive performance results to take a closer look at their situations, examine their respective stories in more detail, and possibly find common characteristics among firms in both ends of the distribution tails (see Chapter 8).

We applied a standard winsorization technique to capture firms with outcomes falling beyond plus or minus three standard deviations from the mean value to identify the performance outliers. This extracted a total of 23 firms with outlier performance including 16 firms in the negative distribution tail and 7 firms in the positive tail of the performance distribution. The firms were subjected to further scrutiny in the form of attempted comparative case studies across these representative (negative and positive) outliers using data and information available from various publicly accessible sources thus adopting a "forensic" approach to analyze these firms. In some cases the firms no longer exist, which makes access to data more challenging and in all instances we were considering events that had taken place over time where access to managerial eyewitnesses were un-accessible. Hence, the analyses attempt to identify distinct similarities among the negative and positive outliers, respectively, and subsequently compare the two groups of firms to note characteristic differences as a way to gain internal validity in findings.

Several of negative outliers are involved in medical equipment development, new technologies, and research-based activities that represent rather risky and capital demanding business activities. Most of the underperforming firms were acquired by successful competitors operating in the same or a related industry. Some firms were delisted from the stock exchange gaining freedom to restructure the business free of the formal information and reporting requirements. Only two of the sixteen firms formally went bankrupt. The firms in the negative performance tail represent growing ventures that push innovative business projects with future earnings potential, but limited flexibility in capital deployment as they manage their investments cautiously in a risky development field. The seven positive outliers operate in diverse businesses including pharmaceuticals, food processing, branded household goods, technology-based products, and environmental solutions. They seem to adapt their business activities in an ongoing incremental manner responding to the changing conditions and prosper from steady responses to emergent market demands supported by unique product-service offerings and flexible response capabilities.

The underperforming firms often associate with negative net income where assets grow slower than the losses thus leading to a higher negative return ratio (ROA). The positive outliers generally display steady increases in profits where assets more or less expand at the same pace, thus maintaining a relatively high return ratio (ROA). Hence, the reported financial returns seem to reflect an ability to manage business expansion in a balanced manner as a noticeable aspect of effective strategic response capabilities.

Discussion

The analyses of comprehensive updated datasets for a 25-year period (1995–2019) reproduced the previously observed left-skewed leptokurtic performance distributions with negative risk-return correlations while observing some nuances across different industry contexts and periodic economic conditions. In this process, we identified adverse effects of executive overconfidence and incentives to manipulate earnings and positive effects associated with structural flexibility that deserve further scrutiny. Considering the influence of adopted accounting practices and automatic statistical relationships between negative skewness in distributions and inverse risk-return correlations, we found similar effects connected to net income and cash flow developments in specific industry contexts. Hence, we do not make any claims that these results validate the theory-based relationships between performance outcomes and risk and vice versa. We merely show that the conventional "Bowman paradox" prevails although it may be caused by other mechanisms than the typically implicated direct causal relationships. To this end, it is found that the computational simulations of a strategic responsiveness model, that depict outcomes from firms with different adaptive capacities, generate the left-skewed performance outcomes and inverse risk-return relations. That is, we show that the commonly observed performance distributions and their peculiar characteristics can derive from heterogeneous adaptive processes across firms. In addition to this, the analyses of extreme negative and positive outliers provide complementary insights.

Hence, we contend that outlying firms in the negative performance tail to a large extent relate to organizations that have struggled in their efforts to respond and adapt to a rapidly changing competitive environment (Fig. 9.3). These firms also represent smaller organizations invested in risky research-driven business

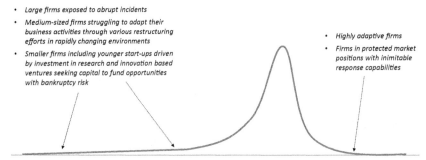

- Large firms exposed to abrupt incidents
- Medium-sized firms struggling to adapt their business activities through various restructuring efforts in rapidly changing environments
- Smaller firms including younger start-ups driven by investment in research and innovation based ventures seeking capital to fund opportunities with bankruptcy risk

- Highly adaptive firms
- Firms in protected market positions with inimitable response capabilities

Fig. 9.3. Summary of Findings Across the Distribution of Performance Outcomes.

development and large firms adversely affected by major risk incidents. The firms in the positive performance tails are generally found to engage in balanced adaptive responses honing the changing demands in the market supported by unique firm-specific resources and capabilities.

Implications for Theory and Practice

The preceding analyses confirm the existence of the "Bowman paradox" as conventionally conceived and measured but do not give credence to direct causal relationships between performance and risk outcomes and vice versa. Instead, computational model simulations find that heterogeneous adaptation across firms appear a more credible driver of the empirically observed performance and risk characteristics. Hence, the observed phenomena of left-skewed performance distributions and inverse risk-return relationships seem to arise, if not entirely then at least partially, from difference in the adaptive processes performed among competing firms and the specific ways in which we measure accounting-based performance and the associated variance-based risk indicators. In turn, the effectiveness of the adaptive organizational processes performed by the firms are influenced by various leadership traits and structural features imposed on the organization and provide relevant insights commensurate with rationales from psychology, behavioral theories, and organizational studies presented in the extant literature.

This suggests that the regularly observed phenomena of left-skewed performance outcomes and inverse risk-return relationships most likely are associated with the adaptive processes assumed by competing firms, for example, a rigid annual budgeting process versus frequent interactive information updating. That is, differences in the way leaders approach internal decision structures and information processing will cause large discrepancies in performance outcomes. So, we can learn more about the strategy-making processes that drive sustainable adaptive outcomes through further studies of effective strategic response capabilities and their structural features.

For practicing managers, this implies that strategic adaptation is, or should be, a central concern because it determines how the firm can elevate its status to become a positive high performer as opposed to a negative underperformer.

Limitations and Future Research

Although the statistical analyses are based on comprehensive datasets we recognize the possibility of spurious effects in the reported findings although the empirical evidence seems to provide strong support for the reported results. Furthermore, the computational simulation model is relatively simple and obviously have shortcomings in its ability to explain multiple effects in minute detail. Nonetheless, the observed model results largely, if not perfectly, resemble the empirical performance data across industries and economic scenarios and thus gain validity from comparisons with the real-life data. The simulations also do not consider concrete accounting practices or the intercompany competitive dynamics, which may partially explain why the modeled outcomes are less than perfect reflections of reality. However, the key characteristics of the empirically observed performance distributions are indeed captured by the model simulations.

The preceding analyses consider important control variables to account for effects of executive overconfidence, accounting manipulation, and structural flexibilities in the organization that typically are taken into account. The existence of executive biases inflicted by overconfidence have real effect on the strategy-making processes adopted by the firms (e.g., Schumacher et al., 2020). The incentive to manipulate the accounts similarly exert significant influences on the accounting-based performance measures we often take for granted (e.g., Schrand & Zechman, 2012). These and other related considerations provide promising venues for more detailed future studies of the adaptive process effects among competing firms.

Conclusion

The computational simulations generated by a simple strategic responsiveness model show that heterogeneous strategy-making processes can generate the commonly observed performance outcomes that produce left-skewed returns and inverse risk-return relations. The heterogeneous aspects of the adaptive processes are associated with structural, cognitive, and behavioral influences as fruitful dimensions for further exploration.

Hence, we see a confluence toward strategic responsiveness processes as the key to understand the empirically observed performance distributions that may serve as promising basis for future studies of effective strategic adaptation. So, effective strategic responsiveness emerges as a central theme in future studies of sustainable adaptive outcomes.

References

Adner, R., & Helfat, C. (2003). Corporate effects and dynamic managerial capabilities. *Strategic Management Journal, 24*(10), 1011–1025.
Albæk, M., & Andersen, T. J. (2021). The distribution of performance data: Consistent evidence of (extreme) negative outcomes. In T. J. Andersen (Ed.), *Strategic responsiveness for a sustainable future: New research international management* (pp. 147–174). Bingley: Emerald Publishing.

Alles, L. A., & Kling, J. L. (1994). Regularities in the variation of skewness in asset returns. *Journal of Financial Research, 17*(3), 427–438.

Andersen, T. J. (2015). Strategic adaptation. In J. D. Wright (Ed.), *International encyclopedia of the social & behavioral sciences* (Vol. 12, pp. 501–507). Amsterdam: Elsevier.

Andersen, T. J. (2021). Dynamic adaptive strategy-making processes for enhanced strategic responsiveness. In T. J. Andersen (Ed.), *Strategic responses for a sustainable future: New research in international management* (pp. 49–65). Bingley: Emerald Publishing.

Andersen, T. J., & Bettis, R. A. (2014). The risk-return outcomes of strategic responsiveness. In T. J. Andersen (Ed.), *Contemporary challenges in risk management* (pp. 63–90). London: Palgrave Macmillan.

Andersen, T. J., & Bettis, R. A. (2015). Exploring longitudinal risk-return relationships. *Strategic Management Journal, 36*(8), 1135–1145.

Andersen, T. J., Denrell, J., & Bettis, R. A. (2007). Strategic responsiveness and Bowman's risk-return paradox. *Strategic Management Journal, 28*, 407–429.

Andersen, T. J., & Schröder, P. W. (2010). *Risk management practice: How to deal effectively with major corporate exposures.* Cambridge: Cambridge University Press.

Bettis, R. A., & Hitt, M. A. (1995). The new competitive landscape. *Strategic Management Journal, 16*, 7–19.

Bloom, N., & Van Reenen, J. (2007). Measuring and explaining management practices across firms and countries. *Quarterly Journal of Economics, 122*(4), 1351–1408.

Boisot, M., & McKelvey, B. (2011). Connectivity, extremes, and adaptation: A power-law perspective of organizational effectiveness. *Journal of Management Inquiry, 20*(2), 119–133.

Bowman, E. H. (1980). *A risk/return paradox for strategic management.* Working Paper No. WP 1107-80. Alfred P. Sloan School of Management, Massachusetts Institute of Technology.

Bowman, E. H. (1981). *The risk/return paradox explored.* Working Paper No. WP 1263-81. Alfred P. Sloan School of Management, Massachusetts Institute of Technology.

Bromiley, P. (1991). Testing a causal model of corporate risk taking and performance. *Academy of Management Journal, 34*(1), 37–59.

Campbell, J. Y., & Hentschel, L. (1992). No news is good news: An asymmetric model of changing volatility in stock returns. *Journal of Financial Economics, 31*, 281–318.

Conrad, J., Dittmar, R. F., & Ghysels, E. (2013). Ex ante skewness and expected stock returns. *Journal of Finance, 68*(1), 85–124.

Di Meoa, F., Larab, J. M. G., & Surroca, J. A. (2017). Managerial entrenchment and earnings management. *Journal of Accounting and Public Policy, 36*, 399–414.

Dichev, I. D., & Tang, V. W. (2009). Earnings volatility and earnings predictability. *Journal of Accounting and Economics, 47*, 160–181.

Dichev, I. D., Graham, J. R., Harvey, C. R., & Rajgopal, S. (2013). Earnings quality: Evidence from the field. *Journal of Accounting and Economics, 56*(2–3), 1–33.

Duffee, G. R. (1995). Stock returns and volatility: A firm-level analysis. *Journal of Financial Economics, 37*(3), 399–420.

Eisenhardt, K. M. (1989). Making fast strategic decisions in high-velocity environments. *Academy of Management Journal, 32*(3), 543–576.

Ekholm, A., & Pasternack, D. (2005). The negative news threshold: An explanation for negative skewness in stock returns. *European Journal of Finance, 11*(6), 511–529.

Fama, E. F., & French, K. R. (1992). The cross section of expected stock returns. *Journal of Finance, 47*, 427–65.

Fama, E. F., & French, K. R. (2000). Forecasting profitability and earnings. *Journal of Business, 73*(2), 161–175.

Fiegenbaum, A., & Thomas, H. (1986). Dynamic and risk measurement perspectives on Bowman's risk-return paradox for strategic management: An empirical study. *Strategic Management Journal, 7*, 395–407.

Fiegenbaum, A., & Thomas, H. (1988). Attitudes toward risk and the risk-return paradox: Prospect theory explanations. *Academy of Management Journal, 31*, 85–106.

Froot, K., Scharfstein D., & Stein J. (1993). Risk management: Coordinating corporate investment and financing policies. *Journal of Finance, 48*(5), 1629–1658.

Goodburn, M. (2015). *What is the life expectancy of your company?* World Economic Forum. Retrieved from https://www.weforum.org/agenda/2015/01/what-is-the-life-expectancy-of-your-company/

Gunny, K. A. (2010). The relation between earnings management using real activities manipulation and future performance: Evidence from meeting earnings benchmarks. *Contemporary Accounting Research, 27*(3), 855–888.

Helfat, C. E. (2007). Stylized facts, empirical research and theory development in management. *Strategic Organization, 5*(2), 185–192.

Henkel, J. (2000). The risk-return fallacy. *Schmalenbach Business Review, 52*, 363–373.

Henkel, J. (2009). The risk-return paradox for strategic management: Disentangling true and spurious effects. *Strategic Management Journal, 30*, 287–303.

Lasi, H., Fettke, P., Kemper, H. G., Feld, T., & Hoffmann, M. (2014). Industry 4.0. *Business & Information Systems Engineering, 6*, 239–242.

McNamara, G., & Bromiley, P. (1997). Decision making in an organizational setting: Cognitive and organizational influences on risk assessment in commercial lending. *Academy of Management Journal, 40*(5), 1063–1088.

McNamara, G., & Bromiley, P. (1999). Risk and return in organizational decision making. *Academy of Management Journal, 42*, 330–339.

Meyer, R., & Kunreuther, H. (2017). *Ostrich paradox: Why we underprepare for disasters.* Philadelphia, PA: Wharton Digital Press.

Nordhaus, W. D. (2011). The economics of tail events with an application to climate change. *Review of Environmental Economics and Policy, 5*(2), 240–257.

Nickel, M. N., & Rodriguez, M. C. (2002). A review of research on the negative accounting relationship between risk and return: Bowman's paradox. *Omega, 30*, 1–18.

Nocco, B. W., & Stultz, R. M. (2006). Enterprise risk management: Theory and practice. *Journal of Applied Corporate Finance, 18*, 8–20.

Ruefli, T. W. (1990). Mean–variance approaches to the risk–return relationship in strategy: Paradox lost. *Management Science, 36*, 368–380.

Ruefli, T. W., & Wiggins, R. R. (1994). When mean square error becomes variance: A comment on "Business risk and return: A test of simultaneous relationships." *Management Science, 40*, 750–759.

Santacruz, L. (2019). Measures of firm risk-taking: Revisiting Bowman's paradox. *Managerial Finance, 46*(3), 421–434.

Schrand, C. M., & Zechman, S. L. C. (2012). Executive overconfidence and slippery slope to financial misreporting. *Journal of Accounting and Economics, 53*(1), 311–329.

Shefrin, H. (2007). Behavioral finance: Biases, mean–variance returns, and risk premiums. *CFA Institute Conference Proceedings Quarterly, 31*, 4–12.

Shefrin, H. (2014). Distinguishing rationality and bias in prices: Implications from judgments of risk and expected return. In T. J. Andersen (Ed.), *Contemporary challenges in risk management: Dealing with risk, uncertainty and the unknown* (pp. 7–49), London: Palgrave Macmillan.

Schumacher, C., Keck, S., & Tang, W. (2020). Biased interpretation of performance feedback: The role of CEO overconfidence. *Strategic Management Journal, 41*(6), 1139–1165.

Taleb, N. N. (2007). *The black swan: The impact of the highly improbable.* New York, NY: Random House.

Teece, D. J., Pisano, G., & Shuen, A. (1997). Dynamic capabilities and strategic management. *Strategic Management Journal, 18*, 509–533.

Teece, D. J. (2007). Explicating dynamic capabilities: The nature and microfoundations of (sustainable) enterprise performance. *Strategic Management Journal, 28*, 1319–1350.

Van der Vegt, G. S., Essens, P., Wahlström, M., & George, G. (2015). Managing risk and resilience. *Academy of Management Journal, 58*(4), 971–980.

Index

Printed in the USA
CPSIA information can be obtained
at www.ICGtesting.com
JSHW010755230224
57903JS00016B/29